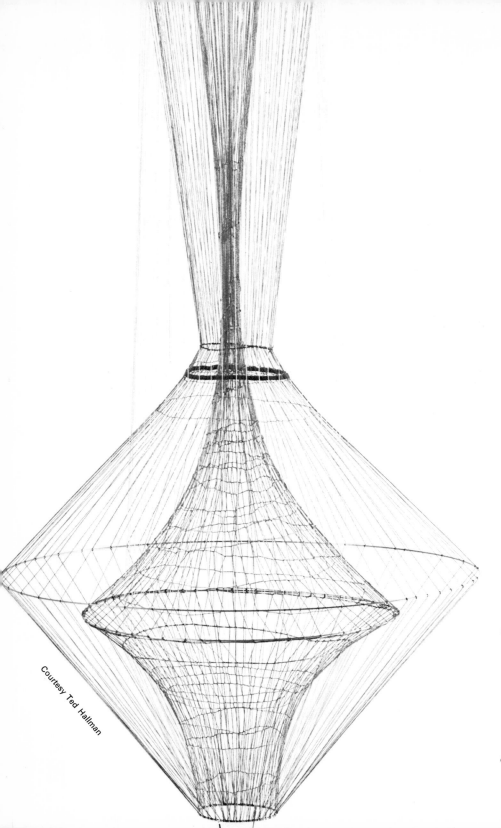

Courtesy Ted Hallman

weaving

without

a loom

sarita r. rainey

art supervisor | montclair | new jersey public schools

davis publications inc. | worcester | massachusetts

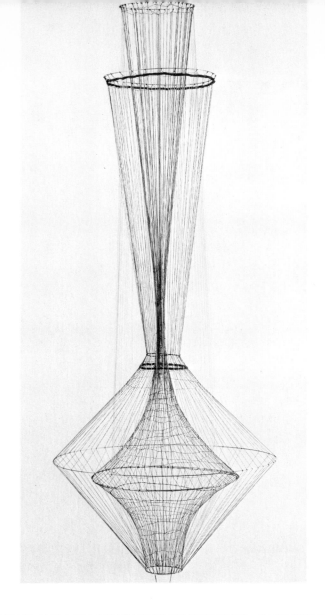

LAYOUT AND TYPOGRAPHY BY JOHN W. CATALDO
ALL PHOTOGRAPHS ARE BY THE AUTHOR UNLESS
OTHERWISE NOTED

THIRD PRINTING—1968

LIBRARY OF CONGRESS CATALOG CARD NUMBER: 65-15254

FOREWORD

Fear and defensiveness seem to have been the major products of our past efforts to interest people in art. We extolled the masterpieces of the great artists and talked awesomely of the "divine spark" that animated their work. The result was that when ordinary people were invited to participate in art, their most frequent reply was, "I couldn't draw a straight line with a ruler."

Sarita Rainey is one of those young art educators who have been working quietly and effectively to show people that they can have meaningful and satisfying experiences with art. An artist in her own right—having exhibited at the Cleveland, Contemporary Crafts, Smithsonian, and other museums—she is equally creative as an educator.

In working with children and teachers, Miss Rainey has been unusually successful in encouraging expression through art, and directing the attention of the individual to his own feelings and thoughts. Furthermore, she has developed many ingenious ways in which beginners can be led to work with art without being frustrated by the technical difficulties involved.

In this book, Miss Rainey reveals how she has made the approach to weaving so easy and natural that children and adults have been inspired to explore the many fascinating possibilities inherent in this form of expression. As neophytes gain experience and confidence, they can take on more ambitious projects. Their products may never grace the walls of a gallery nor be stolen from a museum, but the individuals who made them lead richer lives and make their surroundings more interesting.

Through *Weaving Without A Loom*, Sarita Rainey is opening yet another creative approach through which anyone can have extraordinary experiences with art.

George M. Sharp

Dr. George M. Sharp is Assistant Superintendent of the Instructional Program in Montclair Public Schools, Montclair, New Jersey.

INTRODUCTION

Weaving is an ancient hand art. In common with all of the arts, its beginnings were simple, involving at first only the natural materials at hand. A great deal of time must have passed between the first simple interlacing of fibers to form a fabric and the development of the mechancial loom.

In the following pages Miss Rainey has gathered together some of the techniques and materials with which weaving may be accomplished without the need for a regular loom. She has not attempted to take us back to the beginning of the craft, simulating what may have taken place then, but rather, has drawn her material from the 20th century. She is concerned with adapting weaving techniques for use where it is not practical to introduce mechanical loom weaving.

As our children advance in school, the majority of them seem less and less able to meet their own developing standards in the arts. We frequently find it difficult to teach such subjects as color, texture, and pattern through picture making simply because the struggle centers mainly on drawing. In weaving we have no such obstacle so that the child is free to invent, to combine, and to create his own patterns. In the various sections into which the book is divided, Miss Rainey has suggested some possible uses of the materials without offering specific problems or solutions. Her emphasis is on a creative approach through which she opens new avenues for experimentation and expression.

Dr. Jack Arends is Professor and Head of the Department of Art at the Northern Illinois University in DeKalb, Illinois.

Contents

FRONT COVER: Detail of Interwoven Thread Pattern, by the Author

1
weaving as an art form

Weaving, as usually defined, is the interweaving of threads. As an art form, however, it is much more than this. It is a means of creative expression which allows an imaginative person to recapture the thrill of creativity that the primitive weaver once knew.

Weaving has been, since primitive times, a medium for the artist as well as for the person faced with the practical problem of producing cloth, and in every period of history, both types of weaving have been practiced.

Man first wove a few threads together with the only tools available to him—his fingers. With these he lifted different combinations of warp strands and inserted the weft between the separated warp fibers. He intertwined fibers of various textures to produce patterns, and used color to breathe life into them. Inevitably, new materials led to more sophisticated designs, glowing with exotic color and pulsating with life.

As man developed his skill, he wished to speed the weaving process. Instead of using his fingers to raise each thread, he discovered that he could insert a rod under certain threads and raise all of them at one time. By using more than one rod, he found that patterns could be formed even faster.

Step by step, the loom continued to evolve and become more intricate. A device called the harness was invented to raise and lower the warp threads automatically. Complicated power looms appeared and primitive techniques were laid away to gather dust. However, with all of man's mechanical methods, primitive ways of weaving still survive among some craftsmen in the United States and other countries. In an era of discovery, weaving without the popular harness loom offers new excitement and challenge to those who seek to rediscover the simplicity of this primitive art.

For those who are intrigued by the challenge of weaving without the impressive but impersonal harness loom, less complicated devices may

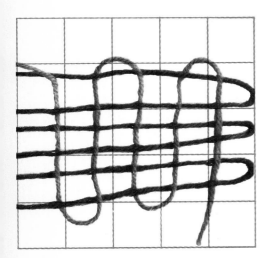

Threads interlaced at right angles.

Loom from Rimac or Lurin Valleys, Peru.

serve for a beginning. A simple frame or background material may be used in place of the harness loom. It is with these and other devices that this book is concerned. Specifically, this book aims to minimize weaving terminology as it explains warp and weft usage; to offer weaving variations; to expand perception; to develop a creative approach with methods and materials; to provide weaving examples for inspiration at all age levels. The devices that have been selected on the basis of their simplicity enable the weaver to develop a personal approach to weaving.

The weaving process can be a challenge to the imaginative worker as he thinks, draws, and constructs with materials. This challenge can stimulate the designer-weaver to make discriminatory decisions in the use of color, texture, and shape; and to expand his perceptions beyond method and technique to the aesthetic. This book illustrates how creative and imaginative weaving on the simplest device provides a challenge to fuse ideas, material and function into an aesthetic whole.

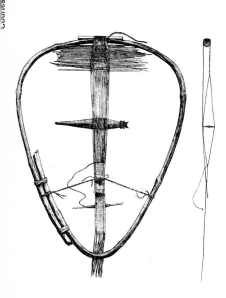

Ucayali Loom of Peru.

Model of a Greek loom. Weights are attached to warp to hold the fibers in place.

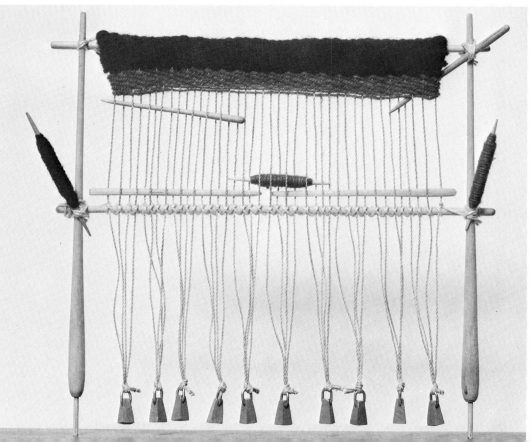

Peruvian Loom showing warp threads attached to rods.

Egyptian weaving shop, Middle Kingdom.   Found near El Giza, Upper Egypt.

Navajo Indian weaving on a primitive loom.

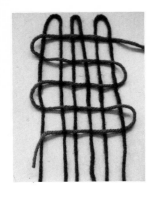

the weaving process:

Interlacing of the threads at right angles to each other.

WARP: vertical threads making the structural "skeleton" for weaving.

WEFT: horizontal fibers woven through the warp.

WARP AND WEFT CONTROL THE DESIGN.

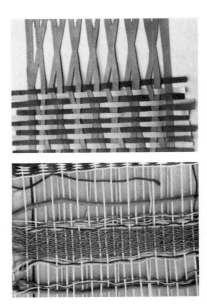

DESIGN: The quality of weaving is determined by color, texture, space, line, shape, and rhythm.   No one of these stands alone; all work together to form a harmonious whole.

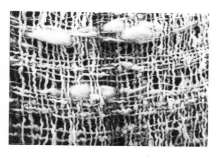

TEXTURE: rough, smooth, soft, hard.

COLOR: inspires, motivates, accents, sets moods, evokes atmosphere.

 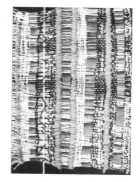 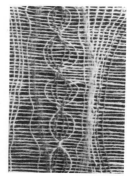

LINE: thick, thin, wide, narrow, for direction, movement, accent.

SPACE: negative (open) or positive (closed)

FORM: outline, filled in, interlocking, overlapping a central figure, the outside shape.

Evelyn Knox

RHYTHM: repetition of color, line, shape, texture.

INSPIRATION may come from many sources, including:

ENVIRONMENT

Man

Animal

Nature

DESIGN

MATERIALS

TECHNIQUES

Yarn is wrapped around warp threads.

Areas of warp threads are painted or dyed before weaving.

Weaving pattern may be varied in many ways.

2 *weaving with paper*

Let's experiment in weaving without a loom. All you need is some imagination and the most readily available material—PAPER. Paper can be a challenge to the ingenuity of any designer-weaver, encouraging endless variations in choice of color, texture, line, and pattern.

Many types of paper may be used for weaving: cellophanes, crepe, metallic, tissue, glazed, blotting, velour, gift, shelf, and wallpapers. Colorful tag boards, paper ribbons, tapes, and even everyday newspaper are also effective. Some papers can be found in scrap piles while others may be purchased from sources such as gift wrapping departments, paper companies, hardware, wallpaper or stationery stores. Collect papers for a period of time before initiating the weaving. Look for colorful and textured papers to stimulate the imagination and inspire ideas. Interesting weaving patterns can be made by using assorted colored papers that range from pastel orchids and pinks to brilliant purples and reds, or by combining rough, smooth, shiny and dull papers.

BASIC MATERIALS
Construction paper of various colors
Poster paper
Scissors
Stapler
Paste

OPTIONAL MATERIALS
X-acto knife
Single edge razor blade
Tag board of various colors
Heavy white paper

Paper weaving can start in kindergarten and proceed through college, each level contributing new and exciting complexities to the craft. The basic operations involved in cutting and weaving warp and weft serve to familiarize the beginner with the weaving process and to develop his appreciation for a simple weaving technique. The advanced student, in turn, can discover more intricate and aesthetic designs by further varying the way warp and weft are cut, varying the way strips of paper are woven, and combining paper weaving with techniques such as block printing and paper sculpture.

procedure

There are a number of ways to cut a sheet of paper so strips may be woven into it. Vertically cut strips act as warp, while horizontal strips are the weft. One easy method for cutting warp involves folding a sheet of paper in half; ruling a line across the paper about a half inch down from the open edges to serve as the margin at top and bottom when opened; and cutting strips of equal or unequal widths, stopping at the margin.

Another method, which may be easier for the young child, makes use of a flat sheet of paper. To make a warp, the margin is marked at the top edge of the paper and strips are cut to that margin. The weft, the strip of paper used for weaving, is passed under-and-over the warp. Alternating the strips so that one strip goes over the warp while the other goes under, will make a tabby pattern and, at the same time, help to hold the weaving together.

THERE ARE UNLIMITED POSSIBILITIES FOR DESIGN IN PAPER WEAVING.

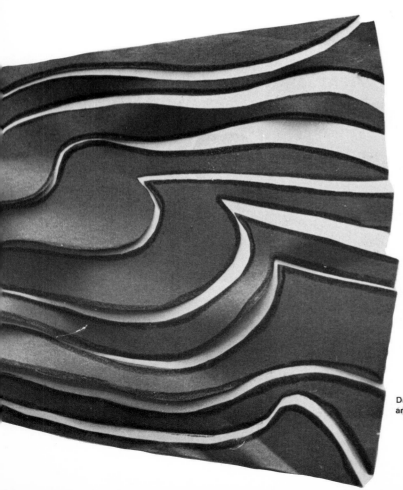

Draw proposed warp lines with crayon
and cut along lines.

Weave through the cut strips.

Paper is cut to form warp.

Slanted slits are cut into a strip of paper; another strip of paper is woven through the slits.

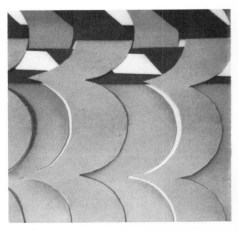

The combined strips are woven as though they were one.

variations

To add variety and interest to paper weaving, experiment with warp and weft. *Make the warp control the design, first cutting strips into shapes, then weaving through them.* For example, cut curved or angular warp strips (Photo A); vary the width of the warp strips for interesting patterns; cut shapes out of, or into, the warp from one or both edges (Photo B). *Make the weft control the design:* Weave over-and-under different combinations of strips (Photo C). For example, weave over-one, under-two, over-three, under-two, or over-one, and under-three; cut parts out of the weft; shape the weft by cutting angular, jagged, or curved lines (Photo F). Weave narrower strips of contrasting colors over previously woven weft (Photo D).

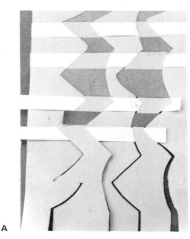

A

Angles and curves cut to form varied warp strips.

D

B

Warp is cut to form irregular shapes; straight strips are woven through them.

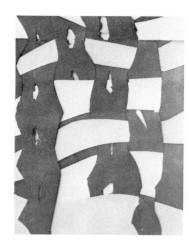

F

Irregular shaped warp and weft.

Try surface enrichments: Paper weaving, whether simple or intricate, must be pleasing and well organized in design before surface enrichments are used. The awareness of basic weaving principles, sensitivity to design, and use of materials are essential to the success of any variation. Paste a narrow strip of contrasting color on top of the weft before using it for weaving. Paste interesting flat or sculptured shapes on top of the squares or rectangles formed by the weaving design. Apply shapes of color and printed text from magazines over certain areas of the weaving, making a collage effect. Weave a form, such as an animal over and into the tabby design, leaving part of the tabby weave for background. Punch holes through the weaving, using a paper punch, then superimpose the weaving over a contrasting paper. Use paint, crayon, yarn, string, or fabric to accent certain woven areas. See next page for examples.

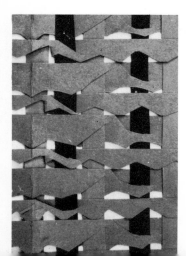

Close-up of finished design.

C

17

Torn paper strips used for warp and weft.

Weaving over and under different combinations of strips.

Sculptured paper pasted on strips of paper.

Paper tied around paper strips.

A block print design is printed on woven

Wet block print is removed from wove

3   *weaving into scrim*

Imaginative patterns can be made by weaving colorful threads into the fabric background of scrim. The fairly large holes in the scrim construction permit thread and yarn to be easily pushed or pulled through the mesh. The design may be changed or rearranged by removing or placing the threads in new positions.

BASIC MATERIALS
Scrim (sometimes called cross-stitch
rug canvas)
Scissors
Yarn or string
Paste and needles

OPTIONAL MATERIALS
Roving (cotton)
Cloth
Weeds

The stiffness of scrim gives body, making it easy to use without a frame and practical for any grade level. A first grader can learn easily the basic technique of over-and-under weaving; older groups and adults can experiment with more diversified techniques.

Beyond the weaving possibilities, scrim can be used as a background for making hooked rugs. This is discussed in a later chapter.

procedure

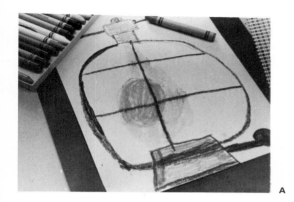
A

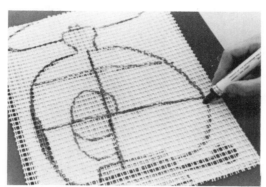
B

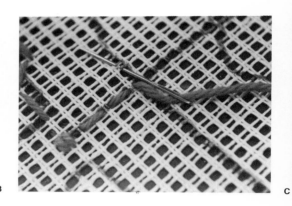
C

WEAVING INTO SCRIM: *Method (1)* Let the shape emerge by weaving spontaneously into the scrim material. *Method (2)* Make a pre-planned design as shown in illustration by outlining the shape on a sheet of paper (Photo A). Place the scrim on top of the paper and use a crayon or felt tip pen to trace over the design, thereby duplicating it (Photo B). Weave over-and-under the scrim fibers as shown in photo C to outline the shape or, with the same weaving procedure, fill in solid areas.

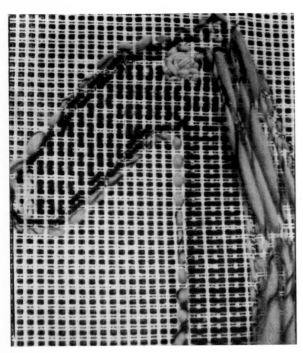

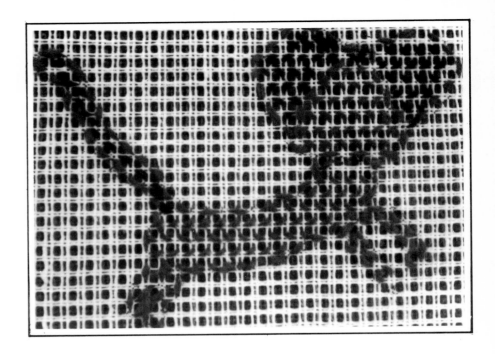

Original designs/Grade 2/Montclair, N.J. Public Schools.

VARIATIONS: Cut out areas and make yarn span open spaces. Overlap yarns to create texture and line. Weave wire of various gauges, tree bark, or cellophane into the scrim. Cut shapes out of scrim to make mobile forms. Combine applique with weaving. Cut pieces of fabric and paste or stitch to the scrim. Superimpose scrim on other backgrounds such as wire mesh and burlap. Combine scrim weaving with rug hooking.

weaving into cotton mesh

4

BASIC MATERIALS
Old picture frame or wood frame
Cotton mesh netting
Stapler
Wool of various colors
Large eye needle
Scissors

OPTIONAL MATERIALS
Pipe cleaners
Raffia
Ribbon
Strings

Many types of cotton mesh provide weaving possibilities, with each offering the designer exciting challenges to experiment with threads and invent a personal weaving method. The mesh serves as a background, with threads woven into the material to form patterns. The design takes shape when yarn is woven under-and-over the threads. As each part of the shape is completed, the design seems to spring to life.

If the designer is resourceful, he will discover that cotton mesh is available in curtains, mosquito netting, onion bags, and dish cloths. It may also be purchased by the yard or collected from scraps. The weaver will need to experiment with different types of mesh to discover the potential of the material.

Collecting unusual materials to weave into the mesh can increase interest and stimulate ideas for more provocative design possibilities. Native materials—grasses, dried flowers, ferns—may be used. Synthetic yarn fibers can further stimulate the weaver by their luxurious colors and textures. Even pipe cleaners can be bent in, around, and through the mesh. As the student works, he will become more alert to mesh materials and their potential for aesthetic expression.

Yarns interwoven into dishcloth—then made into purse by Esther Colton, Vancouver, B.C.

procedures

Mesh, being a flimsy material, works best when fastened to a frame. WOOD FRAME: Use any wood frame, such as a picture frame, to hold the mesh. Cut the mesh a little larger than the opening and attach it to the frame by stapling. CARDBOARD FRAME: Use any heavy cardboard that will not bend when the mesh is stretched tightly over the frame opening. Pieces of corrugated boxes or showcard are effective.

An exciting and challenging way of weaving is to work spontaneously with both material and design. This means weaving directly into the mesh without previous planning. Thread several needles, then experiment with colorful yarns and weaving patterns by changing or rearranging them, until a satisfying pattern emerges. Sometimes a planned design of a single object is desired. For a beginning, follow the accompanying illustrations. Place the frame on paper and draw around the inside of the frame. Attach the mesh to the frame. Create a shape that will fit the size of the frame (Photo A). Place the frame, with mesh face down, on the drawing; the drawing now appears through the mesh. With a crayon or felt marker, follow the lines of the drawing so the dye of the pen will penetrate the mesh (Photo B). The design now shows on the mesh. With a needle and thread, outline and fill in the design (Photo C). Make some lines straight, some wavy, or circular. This will give variety to the finished piece.

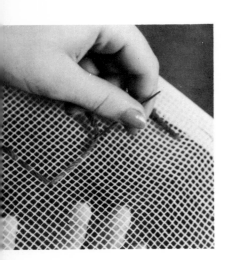

B

C

A

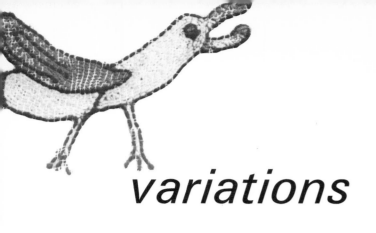

variations

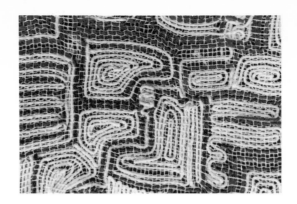

Use the background as part of the design, covering only parts of it with thread or yarn. Combine large, soft yarns with thin, harder ones. Use metallic, shiny materials with dull, smooth ones. Add knots, puffs, or loops to give a different dimension. Superimpose the woven mesh over another fabric or paper. Cut shapes out of the mesh and superimpose it over burlap with pulled threads, then weave colorful yarns into the mesh and burlap. Completed weavings may be stitched together to make a wall hanging by mounting on dowel rods.

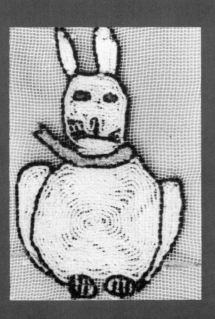

A drawing was made with crayon, then cut out and used as a pattern for drawing the shape on burlap. Colorful yarn was then woven over and under the burlap threads to make the shapes.

Examples by First Graders.

weaving

into burlap

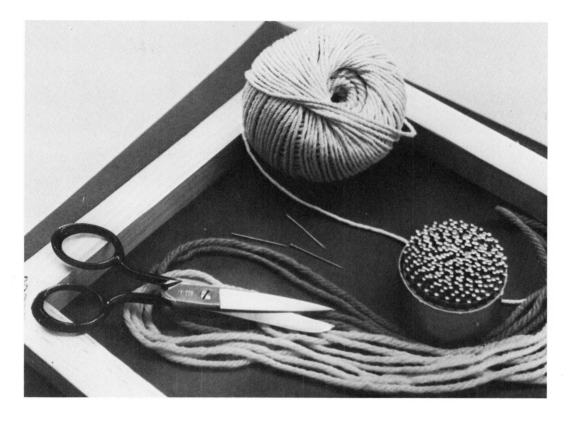

BASIC MATERIALS
Burlap
Yarn
Needles
Scissors
Straight pins
Frame

OPTIONAL MATERIALS
Strings
Fabrics
Cotton
Felt
Velvet
Threads
Reed

Esther Colton/Vancouver, British Columbia.

DESIGNING ON BURLAP: To begin a design, weave colorful string, thread, or yarn in different sets or combinations, such as over-two and under-three burlap threads. This will form a pattern on the burlap. Weave many rows of one combination close together before starting another. Avoid weaving long strands of thread that might appear to be stitchery.

Diagonal needle weaving using embroidery yarn and scrap wool.

27

Burlap impresses children with its texture and color and is an ideal material for weaving as well as for drawn thread techniques. Like scrim and cotton mesh, its threads are so woven that other materials can be woven into it. Similar weaving techniques may be applied to all three materials. While burlap can be purchased by the yard in many beautiful colors, the most practical background colors are natural, hemp, white, or eggshell. Burlap sacks for potatoes and grains also may be used for weaving when washed, pressed, and cut into specific sizes.

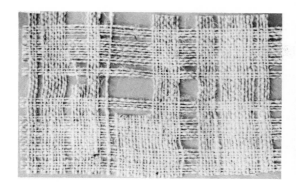

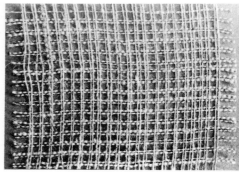

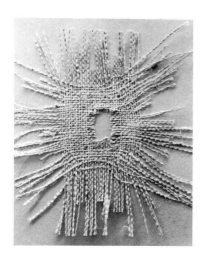

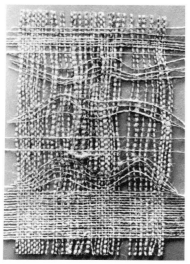

DRAWN THREAD TECHNIQUE: When threads are drawn or rearranged, new compositions emerge. The pulled thread technique, though simple, can trigger unusual designs resulting in wall hangings, draperies, room dividers, or casements and window coverings. New channels of thought aroused through experimentation will promote questions such as the following: What will happen if only weft threads are pulled? Could threads be rearranged to form ovals, curves, and angles? How can textures be effectively used to influence the design?

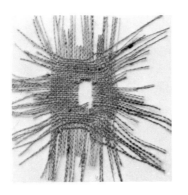 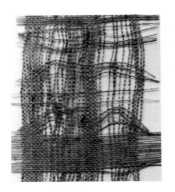 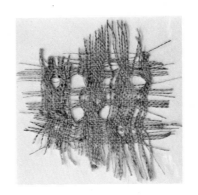 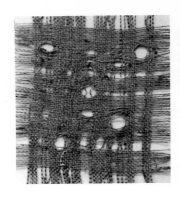

Discover and invent to achieve variety. Pull alternate strands to make a loose weave. Draw strands of threads and move parts of the remaining strands up or down to form curved lines, with the fingers guiding the position of the threads. Pull a series of both warp and weft threads to create open spaces. Pull horizontal threads between sections of unpulled fabric to get an effect of alternate strips.

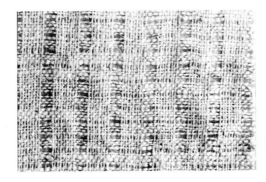  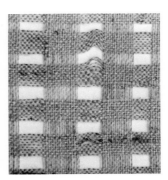

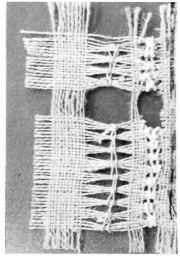

Draw all the horizontal threads, leaving only a band of solid fabric to hold the warp intact, then group the vertical threads together into sections. Remove weft threads and tie the warp threads in groups to form spaces. Pull weft threads partially out, leaving open spaces and a fringe. Weave other threads into the fringe and open design. Weave ravelings into the burlap. The result is an unusual texture and color pattern.

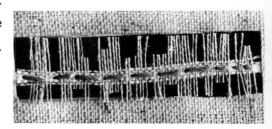

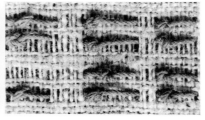

variations

Remember to incorporate design elements that apply to the specific variation. Combine stitchery, applique, or rug hooking with burlap weaving. Superimpose nets or other loosely woven materials over the burlap weaving and then add stitchery to tie the design together. Combine solid areas of burlap weaving with drawn work. Use a variety of printing methods: silk screen, block printing, eraser printing, mono-printing, and potato printing. Make a design with crayon on the burlap. Use stitchery and weaving to add emphasis. Weave colorful yarns through the open spaces resulting from drawn threads.

Cut out area superimposed on another fabric.

Eraser printing on burlap.   Crayon and stitchery.   Potato printing.

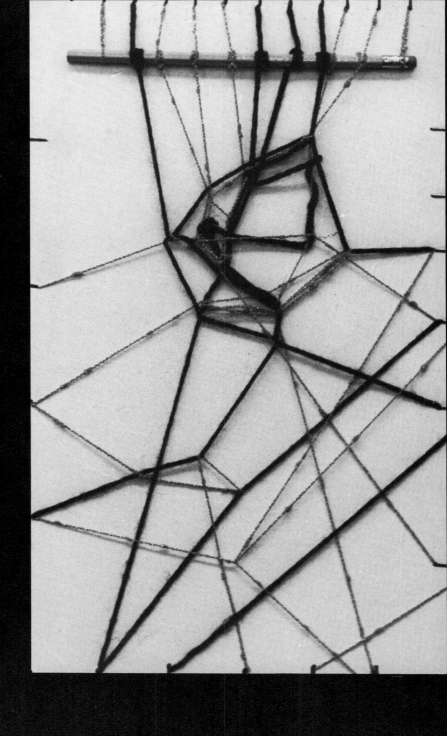

6

ng on a pencil

BASIC MATERIALS
Pencil, ruler, dowel, or broom handle
Yarns of assorted colors and textures
(preferably heavy yarns)
Scissors

OPTIONAL MATERIALS
Raffia
Twine
Plastic gimp
String
Roving
Ribbon
Leather
Adhesive such as ''tri-tex''

A weaving process need not be complicated or expensive to be successful and effective. Rich experiences in design are possible with common, inexpensive materials. The pencil, separated from its familiar context, can become the vehicle for a simple weaving process. Its use is related to the early looms which consisted of nothing more elaborate than warp threads tied to a beam. In pencil weaving, warp fibers are attached to the pencil and the weaver uses his fingers as tools.

Familiarity with additional rod-type objects such as the dowel and broom handle may encourage other experiments and ideas.

procedure

To begin pencil weaving, first decide on the length of the proposed form. Since later in the weaving process the warp strands are woven over-and-under one another, cut strands of yarn approximately one and a half times the length of the planned weaving.

Loop the yarn so that it has a short and long tail and follow the procedure indicated in the photographs.

Loop the yarn so it has a short and long tail and place the pencil across the loop.

Fold the top part of the loop over the pencil.

Pull the short and long ends of the warp thread through the loop and pull tight. This holds the thread on the pencil by forming a knot.

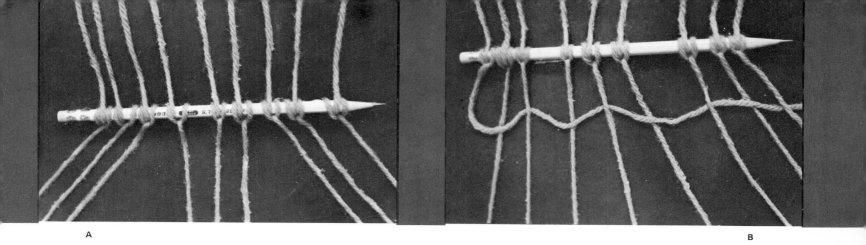

A B

The threads on each end of the pencil will later be used as the weft. To avoid confusion, these should be different in color from the other warp threads (Photo A). The six-inch tails can be put under a book or other heavy object to hold them and the pencil in place during the weaving.

Beginning at the left of the warp, weave the first end thread over-and-under all the way to the right (Photo B). The end thread on the right is then woven back to the left (Photo C). The second thread on the left is woven through to the right. The second thread at the right is then brought down and woven back to the left. The third thread is then used for weaving (Photo D). When the weaving is completed, the ends are knotted in pairs. The loops are then removed from the pencil and knotted in the same manner.

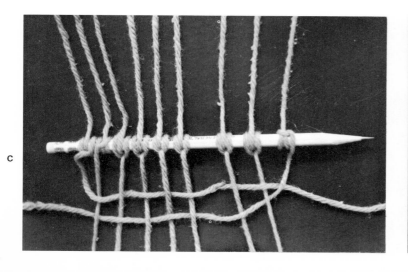

C

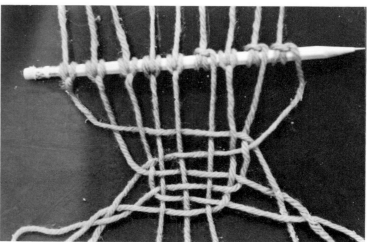

D

variations

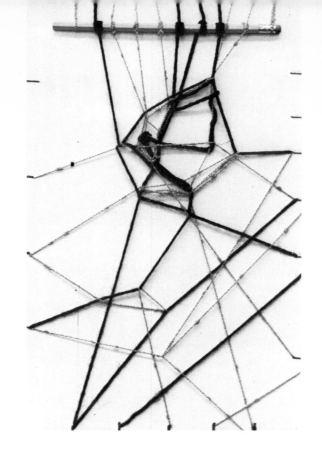

Slender forms are not the only ones which can evolve with pencil weaving. One can make wider forms by varying the number of warp strands and the length of the pencil or rod. Simple or intricate designs result when thin and thick yarns are used together; when tabby and tapestry techniques are combined in the same design; or when finished forms are stitched together to make a single shape.

Pencil weaving assumes another dimension when the pencil is attached to cardboard and the warp threads are stretched to produce a spider web design. This may be done by tying the warp to the pencil, using the same basic procedure previously described. Cut slits on all edges of a piece of cardboard at regular intervals. Place the pencil slightly below the slits on the top edge. Anchor the short ends of the warp in the top slits and long strands at different positions in the side slits. By pulling the warp threads in different directions, the weaver creates a pattern similar to a spider web. Rearrange the threads in different slits to change the design.

To finish the weaving, remove the pencil, leaving the spider web pattern on the cardboard. The completed work is even more effective if the color of the original yarn design contrasts with that of the cardboard. It may also be placed in a mat or frame, or removed and superimposed on a fabric background.

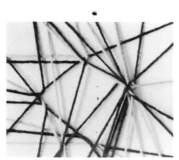

Examples of spider web effect.

Warp tied to broom handle.

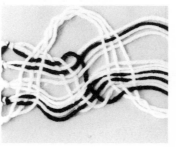

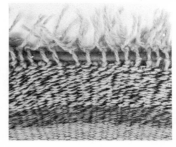

By weaving loosely and permitting spaces to develop between the intertwined threads, the final result will be a woven form.   Detail of finished piece on broom handle.

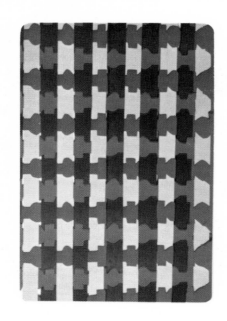

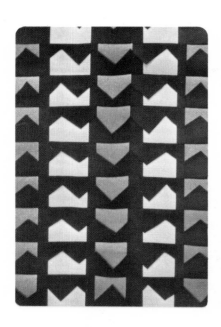

paper weaving

Grade 2

weaving into scrim
and wire

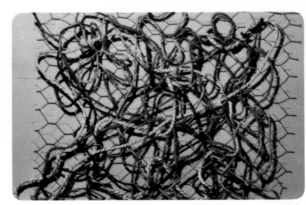

Grade 4

weaving into cotton mesh

Grade 3

Grade 4

Grade 4

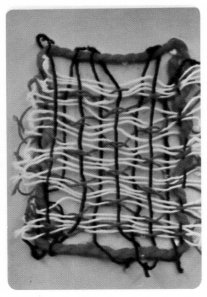

Example of finished piece when cardboard is slit on four sides.

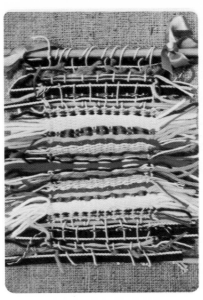

Weft threads used as side fringes; grade 6.

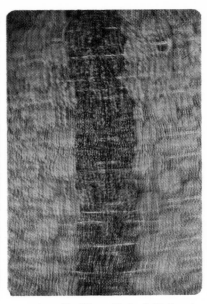

Weaving with different kinds of silk thread.

cardboard weaving

Purse woven on cardboard; college student.

Detail of texture and design in purse at left.

Afghan made from cardboard weavings; grade 4 class.

Woven form with exposed warp threads; college level.

Form made by slitting cardboard on four sides; grade 3.

weaving on drinking straws

Forms woven on drinking straws; grad

weaving on wood frame

Grade 6

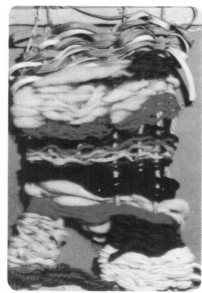

Grade 6

College level

Grade 6

43

weaving with material from nature

44

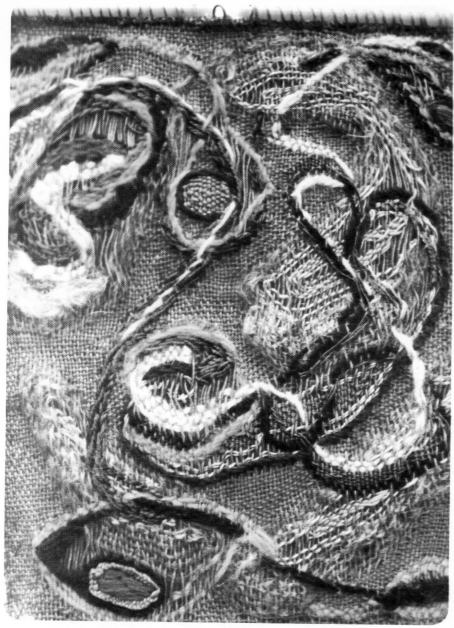

Pulled and woven threads with stitchery, mounted on glass rods; college level.

Pulled and tied threads with weaving and stitchery.

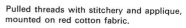

Pulled threads with stitchery and applique, mounted on red cotton fabric.

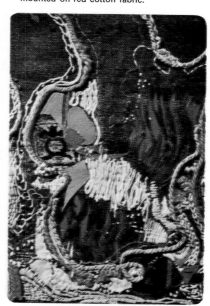

Top and bottom photos by students of Anna Ballarian. San Jose State College, California.

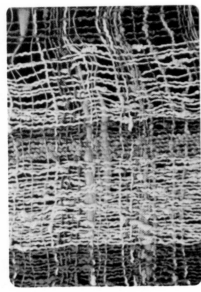

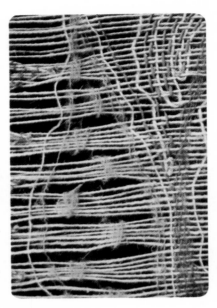

textures and weaves

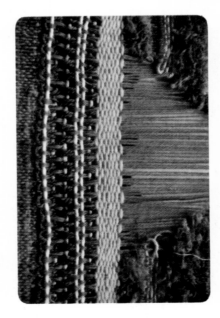

Rug by Jack Arends, Northern Illinois University, DeKalb.

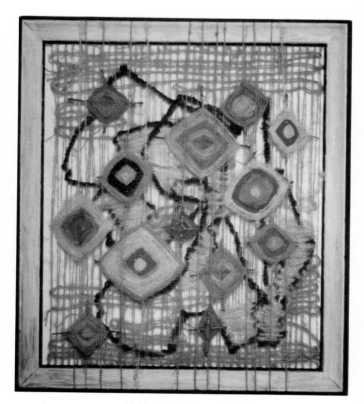

Wall hanging by the author.

Warp made with fishing line.

Weaving with yarns and sticks.

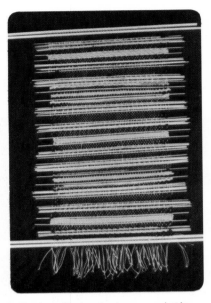

Weaving with dowel rods, yarn, and string.

Weaving decorates a pillow cover.

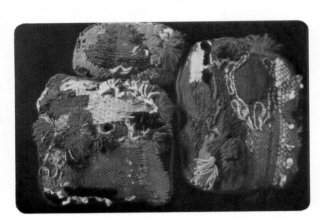

Warp is stitched along top and bottom edges of pillows; strings and yarns are woven through the warp.

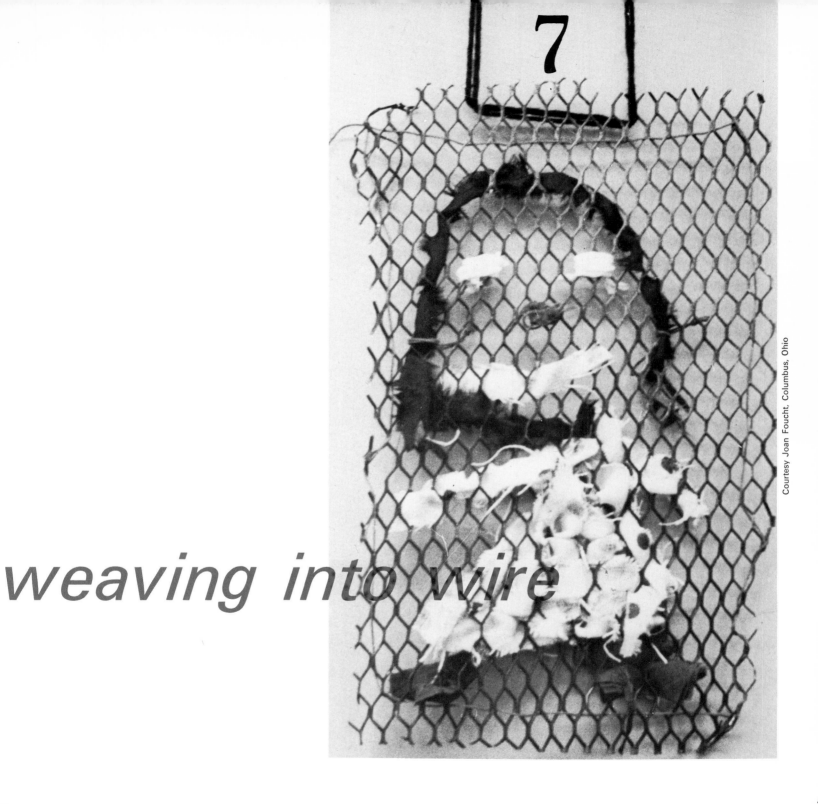

weaving into wire

BASIC MATERIALS: Wire screen; Screen mesh such as window screen; Hardware cloth (large square mesh); Chicken wire; Yarn, String, Wire cutters, Scissors, Needles, Masking tape

OPTIONAL MATERIALS: Burlap, Straw, Beads, Ribbon, Lace, Cellophane, Wools, Pipe cleaners, Tissue paper, Weeds, Felt, Raffia

Weaving in wire mesh, using a variety of types and strips of fabrics, opens fresh new avenues of creative expression. Since wire comes in various meshes, the designer can choose the size of mesh that will best serve his artistic intent. He can manipulate the wire into three-dimensional shapes, cut out parts, or (to create a multi-dimensional effect) superimpose cut-out areas over a screen of different mesh.

The designer should become aware that wire meshes of many types surround him, and each has possibilities and limitations as a background for weaving. In addition, he should be sensitive to color, texture, and pattern; and, considering their potential at each point in design development, use the wire and the surface enrichment to integrate as a pleasing whole. The simple over-under process of weaving into mesh can result in unusual and effective designs as the weaver experiments and explores with aesthetic qualities in mind. Thus, the designer-weaver may give expression to his ideas in many different directions, using a variety of materials, tools and weaving patterns.

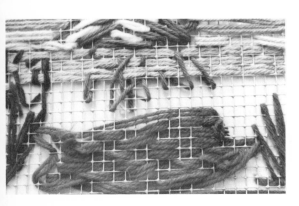

Yarn and string woven in and out through hardware cloth/Grade 1.

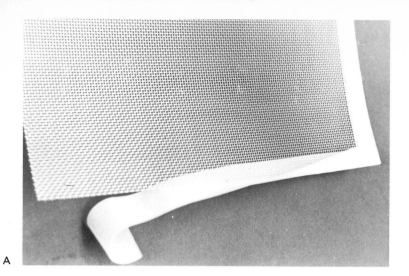

A

D

B

C

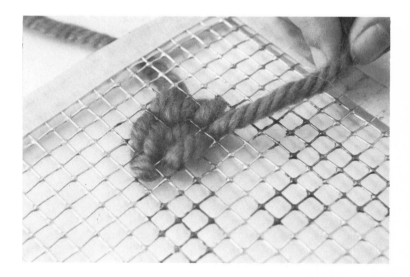

PROCEDURE: An inquiring mind will prove most productive as the weaver searches for new ideas and ways of handling materials. Feel the screen mesh, yarn, string and fabric. See how the materials suggest ideas for weaving. What can you do with wire mesh that is different from scrim or cotton mesh?

Cut the wire and bind it with masking tape to prevent scratches (Photo A). Begin to weave materials into the mesh background. As the weaving progresses, analyze the weaving for design qualities. View it from a distance, or, if a sculptural form, at different angles. Does the design fit the space? Are the colors and textures repeated to make the design a pleasing unit? Are the weaving patterns that go over-and-under the wires varied enough to make a pleasing design?

Using a pre-planned design is another way to begin a weaving. One procedure suggested involves placing the wire shape on paper and drawing around it (Photo B). With a crayon, draw a design on the paper (Photo C). Place the wire mesh over the design. With a felt marker, trace the design to duplicate it on the wire (Photo D).

pattern and texture

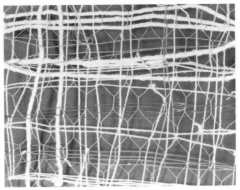

variations

A

PATTERN AND TEXTURE: The use of single strands of yarn makes one type of pattern, while double or triple strands result in still other designs. Interesting surface treatments are suggested by the use of a variety of materials—weeds, unique threads, and different types of yarn.   Leaving areas of wire exposed will vary the pattern and add to the over-all design.

ACCENT: Wool or cotton yarns often need other materials for accent. Raffia may be woven into the mesh to add colorful and textural pattern (Photo A). Roving, a course cotton fiber, can also give dramatic textural quality (Photo B).

The possibilities inherent in this technique are limited only by imagination, and range from simple, expressive forms made by the child to room dividers, wall hangings and sculptural forms reflecting the experience and skill of the professional adult.

Experiments may begin with one of the three most common wire meshes. Chicken wire is highly useful as a background for spanning and connecting areas of yarn by tying or weaving fibers in or around the wire.

Window screen, a fine mesh, encourages the use of threads and finely textured yarns for designing.   Hardware cloth suggests the use of thick yarns and bulky fabrics.   Each wire mesh can be accented by using paint sprays of gold or bronze. Weaving and fabric applique can also be combined when designing in mesh.

B

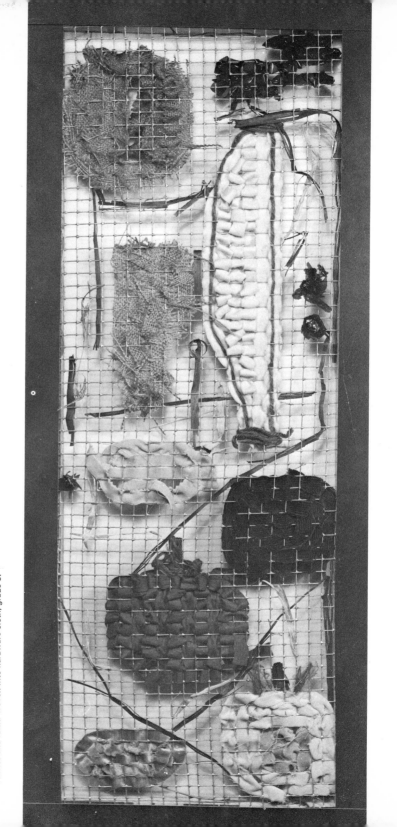

Yarns woven into window screen, grade 6. Teacher, Gwendolyn Thompson.

Fabrics and raffia woven into hardware cloth, grade 3.

53

BASIC MATERIALS
Straws (drinking or soda)
Scissors
String
Yarn

OPTIONAL MATERIALS
Thick and thin yarns
Tinsel
Fabric cut into strips
Ribbon
Nylons cut into strips
Cords

WEAVING

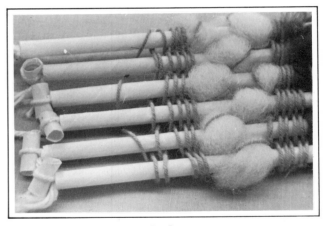

with drinking straws

The every-day drinking straw offers the weaver an opportunity to become acquainted with yet another process that requires no mechanical loom. He learns that straws can be the framework to hold the warp. Narrow or wide forms, made by using varied numbers of straws as the framework to hold the warp, may be woven into colorful belts, ingenious ties, and striking wall hangings.

PROCEDURE: For straw weaving, cut drinking straws in half and cut one warp string for each straw. Strings should be equal in length and as long as the finished product will be. Tie all the warp strings together in a knot. Place the knotted end of warp at the top of the straws, then thread each string through a separate straw. Suck on the straw to get the string through easily. Push the straws up to the knotted ends (Photo A). Weave over and under the straws, beginning a pattern (Photos B and C). Add new color by tying a knot to the previous color and continue the weaving. As the weaving progresses, push the woven section up and off the straws, freeing them for more weaving (Photo D). Slip the straws off the warp when the weaving is finished. Weave the end strings into one another so they will not ravel.

VARIATIONS: Use several strands of warp through each straw. Since this provides for additional warp threads, more intricate weaving is possible. Vary the materials used for weft, using some of the optional materials suggested at the beginning of this chapter. Use pieces of straw as part of the finished design. Sew completed pieces into new forms, or superimpose them on a burlap background.

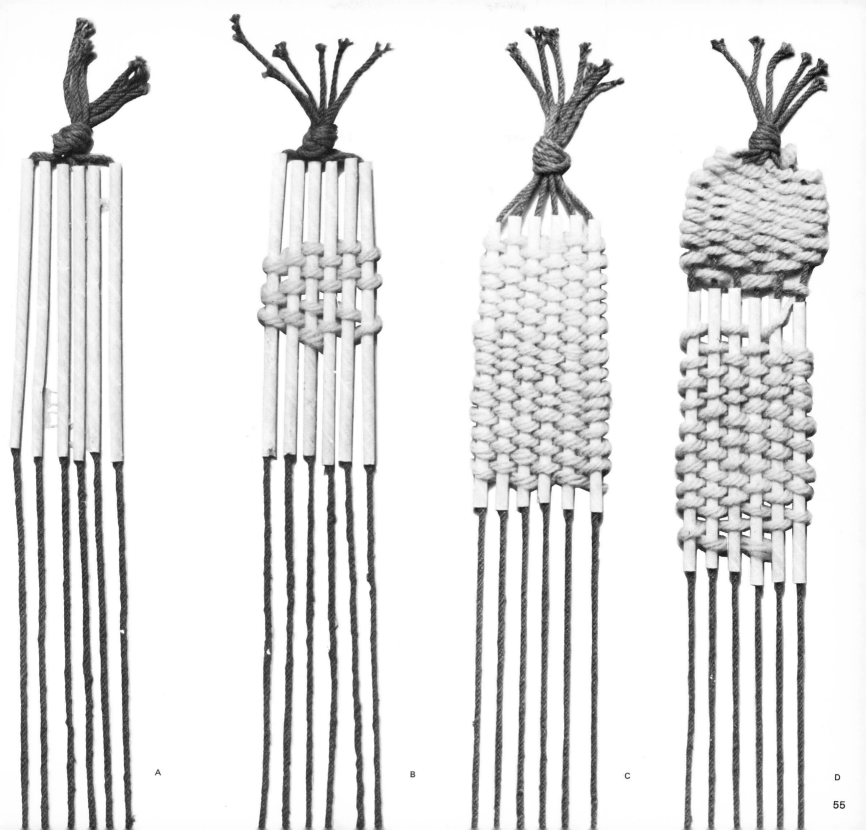

Reed, yarn, and grass used as weft.   Courtesy Youldon Howell, Pasadena City College, Pasadena, California.

Necklace at right was made on cardboard. Warp strands were knotted at top and bottom to make the fringe. A reed was slipped through the top to hold the necklace flat. Side fringe was made from strands of unwoven weft.

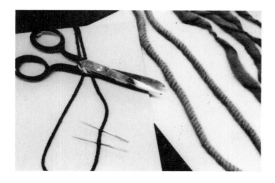

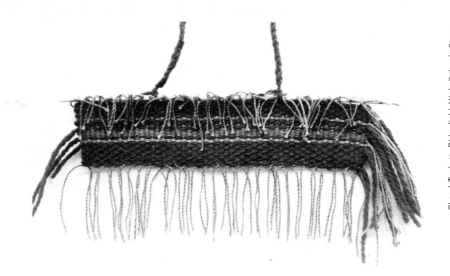

Cheryl Tackett, Ridgefield High School, Conn.

BASIC MATERIALS
Heavy cardboard
String
Yarn
Scissors
Ruler

OPTIONAL MATERIALS
Ribbon
Raffia
Crepe paper
Tissue paper

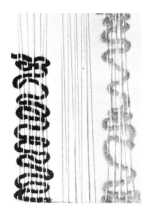

Warp threads are grouped to vary pattern.

weaving on cardboard

While the use of a piece of cardboard to stretch warp is traditional, its practicability and economy still intrigue the experimental weaver. There are many advantages inherent in this form of weaving. The cardboard can be cut into various shapes and sizes. The warp and weft are easily rearranged as the designer experiments. The cardboard may remain as backing for the completed weaving, or the weaving can be removed from the cardboard and displayed as a woven form. Several pieces of cardboard weaving may be stitched together to make a wall hanging, afghan, or rug. Finally, experimental pieces woven on cardboard make a base for planning larger weavings. The cardboard technique, plus a little imagination, opens exciting new avenues of expression.

The design of the weaving should not be limited to row after row of color in a tabby weave. The designer will want to expand his thinking to include the emotional impact of color that may be cool, warm, vivid, or somber; the relationship of color and texture; the possibilities of textural combinations; and the effects to be gained from using varied weaving techniques. Dealing with tactile materials encourages expression through texture.

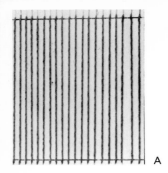

A

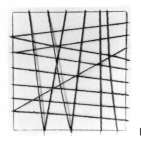

B

procedure

Each length of the warp may be looped around the teeth formed by the slits so that the warp lies flat on the front surface of the cardboard. Do not pull the string too taut, or the cardboard will buckle when weaving.

Courtesy John Lidstone. Photo Roger Kerkham.

THREADS

The warp threads running from top to bottom of the cardboard provide the structural skeleton for the weaving operation (Photo A). It may be superimposed on cardboard and anchored in slits, or held in position by a cardboard frame (Photo C). The arrangement of the structural skeleton definitely influences the final design. Any rearrangement of the warp changes the ultimate pattern of the piece being woven.

Suggested here are two methods of placing warp on cardboard. In one, no frame is needed. To use this method, draw a line along the top and bottom of the cardboard about a half inch from the edge. Cut slits from edge to this line, about a half inch apart. Anchor the warp in the top slits, and stretch the fibers to the bottom of the cardboard (Photo A). The second method is to attach the warp to a cardboard frame. This permits working from both front and back of the weaving. Cut four strips of cardboard. Make slits in the two pieces used for top and bottom of

the frame, being sure that there is an equal number of slits on each side. Next, staple the four pieces of cardboard together, pointing slits outward so that they serve as serrations through which the warp can be looped. Pull the warp just tight enough so that it will lie flat on the frame (Photo C).

The simplest way to arrange the warp is to space the threads at equal intervals. However, placing the warp strands at unequal distances from one another lends variety and interest. It is here that the student is free to experiment and discover new and varied weaves. Still another kind of pattern and more intricate method makes use of cut slits in the sides as well as the top and bottom of the cardboard (Photo B).

WEFT: Horizontal threads (the weft) add flesh to the structural skeleton as they are woven over-and-under the warp. Combining different weaves or techniques, the weaver is able to create unusual and attractive patterns by his inventive use of weft.

Strips of fabric serve as weft.

Courtesy John Lidstone.
Photo, Roger Kerkham.

Purse made by weaving on two pieces of cardboard then stitching the forms together. Handle added to top; woven edge folded over portion of handle and stitched.

Patricia Palmieri

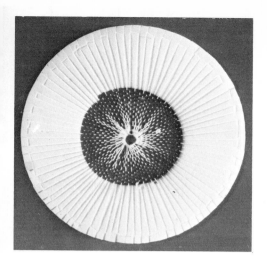

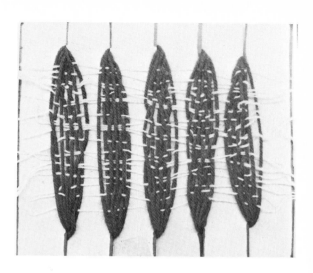

Circle of cardboard is slit around edges and a hole placed in the center. Warp is anchored in slits and wrapped around both sides of the circle.

Woven form made on cardboard circle. Later this piece was mounted on burlap wallpaper with wood molding at top and bottom. Student, Ridgefield High School, Conn.

Warp woven several times through each slit in top and bottom edges of cardboard. Design completed by weaving weft threads through warp.

Warp wrapped around both sides of cardboard. Horizontal threads also woven around both sides of cardboard. Top edge of the weaving left open so form can be slipped off the cardboard. The result is pocket effect or purse. Loose threads at top can be folded over and hemmed, then a lining made and fitted to inside.

Different kinds of cardboard forms make unusual purse shapes. To remove weaving from an intricate shape such as this one, the cardboard must be bent before shape is slipped off. Eileen M. Scally.

Tissue paper combined with yarn serves as weft material. College Student.

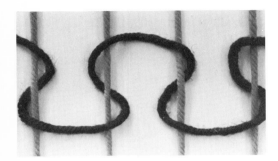

variations

FRAME: Cut slits in the edges of the cover of a shoe box or gift box. Anchor the warp in the slits, then stretch it across the box top. The result is a shadow box effect with the design varying according to the depth of lid and slits. Use a variety of cardboard shapes to obtain interesting forms. A collar shaped cardboard, for example, is a useful base for weaving yarns and beads into collars and jewelry necklines.

WARP: Use different warp arrangements, or tie some of the warp strings together, leaving open spaces. Weave other areas solid.

WEFT: Experiment with different loop techniques. Try weaving yarn of contrasting color between two warp strands, carrying it in back of the tabby weaving and over the front to form a loop. Another loop technique begins with a tabby weave (over-and-under the alternate warp threads). Loops are formed by lifting the weft of alternate warp threads and inserting a rod, stick or brush handle. Weaving several more rows of tabby will hold the loops in place when the rod is removed. Experiment with unusual weft materials. Try combining tissue paper, wool, and string. Use strips of synthetic leathers, reed, cords, and dried grasses. Search through scraps and nature sources.

Close-up of process.

Box top with yarn pulled through slits on all four sides. Corinne Winters, College Student.

Cardboard weaving done with a needle.
Mary Thomas, Maplewood, N. J.

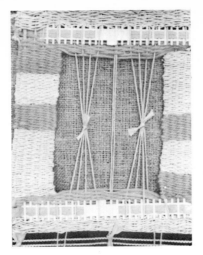

Middle warp strings tied and entire weaving mounted on burlap background.

Weaving made by cutting animal shape from cardboard.

Slits made around the edges hold the warp.

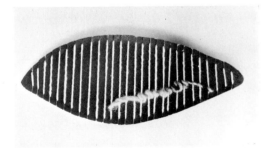

Cardboard shape ready for weaving.

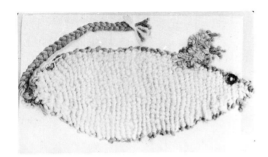

Weaving completed.

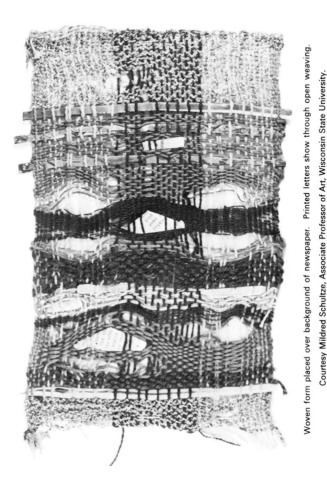

Woven form placed over background of newspaper. Printed letters show through open weaving.
Courtesy Mildred Schultze, Associate Professor of Art, Wisconsin State University.

Elephant shape of wool and nylon hose, woven on cardboard.

61

10
weaving on a frame

BASIC MATERIALS
Strips of wood
Hammer
Nails
String
Yarn
OPTIONAL MATERIALS
A discarded wood frame
Fishing line
Reed
Nylon
Weeds

Frames have been used for centuries when a more precise form of weaving was desired. Primitive weavers used many devices, some similar to the Peruvian frame shown in Chapter one, to weave the cloth they needed.

Pearl Greenberg, Downtown Community School. Photo Murray Greenberg.

A

B

Design made with jute.

Courtesy Lily Mills, Shelby, North Carolina.

Frames suitable for weaving may be of cardboard, as suggested in a previous chapter, or strips of wood. They may be picture frames made of soft wood, stretcher frames used for oil painting (Photo B), or simple handmade frames. They may be commercially designed specifically for weaving (Photo C); or, on the other hand, they may be such ingenious devices as beach chairs turned upsidedown (Photo A).

Forked tree branch used as a frame, by junior high school student, Montclair, N. J. Warp is stretched from one arm of branch to another, thus making an irregular background.

procedure

Weaving on frames has several significant advantages, among which are their availability and versatility. Frames need not follow a set pattern, but may be made in different shapes.

To make a handmade frame, cut two equal lengths of soft wood for the top and bottom of the frame and two longer pieces for the sides. Brads or corrugated fasteners hammered in at the corners will hold the frame together. Drive small nails at equal intervals along the top and bottom strips. Tie the warp to the first nail at the top, pull it down and around the first nail at the bottom, and up again to the next top nail, stretching the warp top to bottom until all the nails are used (Photo A). Once the warp has been stretched, the designer is ready to weave.

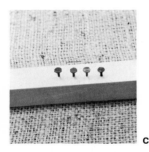

Nails arranged into patterns, either equally or unequally spaced, lay a precise groundwork for the final weaving (Photo B). Different kinds of carpet tacks and staples may be used (Photos C & D). The frame may be more than a device for weaving, since it may be used as an integral part of the weaving design.

After deciding on the type and shape of the frame, the weaver should be concerned with the specific material used for weaving. Treating threads and yarns as color and texture helps the inventive designer to perceive with new sensitivity as he creates woven compositions. He will innovate, experiment, and explore a vast range of materials, from the traditional to the new synthetics.

C

The creative weaver will avoid monotonous strips of color and tabby weave and use imaginative approaches to design and technique. He will explore textural combinations to give variety to his design using materials such as yarn, straw, nylon stockings, and weeds; try different pattern formations which include weaving over-two threads, under-one; be creative with color combinations, using one color with another or interlocking color as in the tapestry technique; and experiment with special relationships, such as combining open areas with solidly woven areas.

D

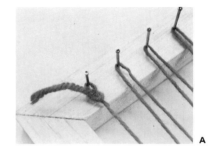
A

B

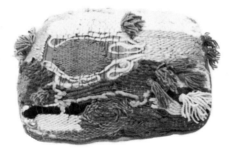

Weaving removed from frame and used for cushion top.

Grade 3. Courtesy Montclair Public Schools, Montclair, N.J.

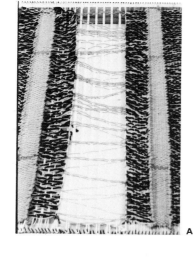

A

Using the warp as part of the design, weave one section at a time. Make one section a tight weave and the others more loose; or let the warp alone be the design for the center, giving an airy effect (Photo A). Insert dowel rods to raise and lower the warp strands under different sets of fibers (Photo B). Experiment with tapestry variations. Explore triangular or hexagonal frames. Make a frame in separate sections fitted together for large, unusual shapes. Use an orange crate as a frame. Place nails at each end, notch the wood, and loop the yarn around the notches. Imaginative designs are possible.

Design made with string woven on an orange crate.

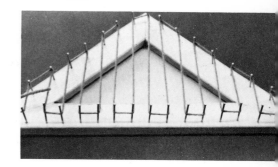

B

Dowel rods are used to raise the warp. Drawer or box may be used as a structure to hold the warp.

Made on sectional frame fitted together to form shape. College level.

Cardboard frames.

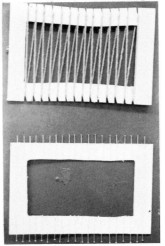

Warp held in place by notches.

Warp held in place by straight pins.

Handmade frames.   Photo courtesy Naomi Dietz.

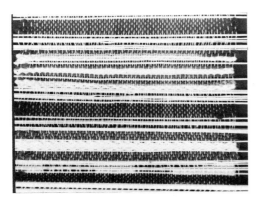

Thin dowel rods woven through warp.

Strips of burlap and yarn woven through warp strings. Nancy Owens

Fishing line used for warp and fringe.

66

mounting

A

Transfer the weaving from the frame to dowel rods. Carefully remove the warp from the nails at one end and push the dowel through the series of loops (Photo A). Then remove the warp at the other end and place a dowel through those loops. The weight of the dowels causes the finished piece to hang straight and yet remain flat. If more weight is needed, small metal weights may be purchased from sewing shops or hardware stores. Attach the weight at the bottom end behind the piece, then cover it with a strip of material to give the weaving a neat appearance.

Weaving also may remain mounted on the original work frame (Photo B) and molding attached to it; or be placed in a picture frame or on mat board.

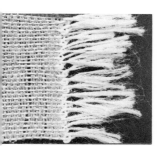

Each warp string was looped to form a loose knot, then strands of the string separated to make fringe.

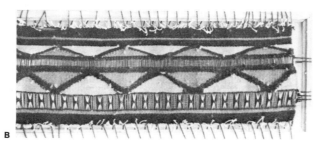

B

Warp was wrapped around 300 finishing nails to form design.

Purse made on rectangular frame with binders twine and strips of leather. Woven piece removed from frame and folded in half to make purse shape. Gale Youngworth.

Courtesy Mildred Haskens, Indianapolis, Indiana

Strings and yarn woven on a wood frame.   Warp threads distorted to develop woven form and finished piece mounted on burlap.

Student work.   Courtesy Marilyn R. Pappas, Miami-Dade Jr. College, Florida

weaving with reed 11

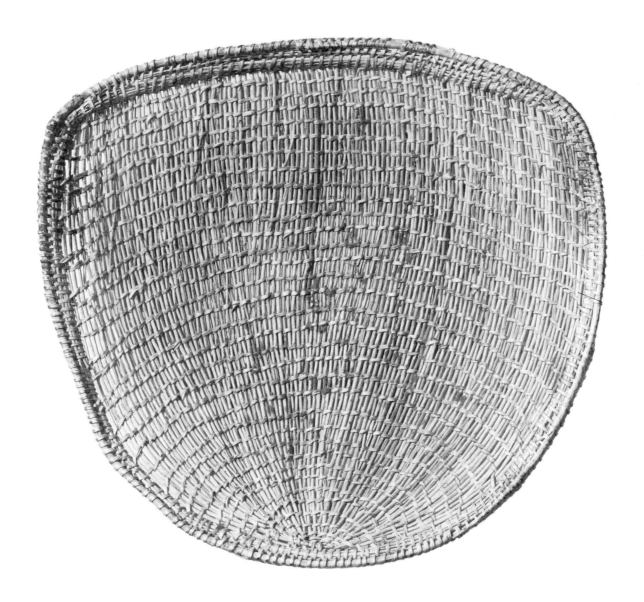

Papajo coil basket, Arizona.   Courtesy American Museum of Natural History, New York City

BASIC MATERIALS

Sponge—to dampen reed and take up excess water
Pan for water—to soak reed
Pincers or pliers—to hold or bend curved areas
Scissors
Ruler or tape measure—to measure lengths of reed
Pencil—to mark measurements
Sandpaper—to smooth rough areas when finished and dry
Pen knife
Round and flat reed

OPTIONAL MATERIALS

Rattan
Raffia
Cords
Strings and twines

NATIVE MATERIALS

Twigs
Vines
Grasses
Pine needles
Corn husks
Cattails
Mosses
Stems
Leaves
Bark

PAPERS

Crepe paper
Tissue paper
Cellophane

MATERIALS USED BY
AMERICAN INDIANS

White oak and River reed

From the collection of Harold Krevolin.
Photo by Robert Tuccio.

weaving with reed

Reed offers another dimension to the possibilities of weaving without a loom. While commonly used for contemporary items such as place mats, room dividers, door mats, purses, decorative animals and the ubiquitous basket, reed weaving has not been developed fully as an art form. Even in the school curriculm, use of reed is often limited to the making of traditional and often unaesthetic baskets. The potential of this material should challenge the designer-weaver to seek new directions that will transform reed into imaginative baskets, exciting two and three dimensional woven shapes, wall hangings and sculptural forms.

The basic basketry process, one of the oldest methods of weaving, should not be disregarded by the contemporary weaver of reed. Basketry techniques of weaving and decorating are useful when applied to experimental reed weaving. These techniques can be the beginnings for a base which, when varied, may emerge as a striking shape or mobile. Even the decorative materials used in early basketry can inspire the designer-weaver of today: stones, shells, teeth, feathers, porcupine quills. Natural dyes from seeds, fruits, and roots, and many other sources add interest and color.

More than sixty years ago in his book *Indian Basketry*, Otis Mason said that the basket maker "...must be botanist, colourist, weaver, designer, and poet, all in one." This is still true of the weaver of reed. As a botanist, he must explore his surroundings in search of materials; as a colourist, he must know which plants, seeds, and juices make dramatic natural dyes; as a weaver, he must experiment with variation and repetition of weave; as a designer, he must assemble and develop forms and patterns that enhance each other; and as poet, he must synthesize the parts into an aesthetic whole.

Sculptural form. Grade 6.

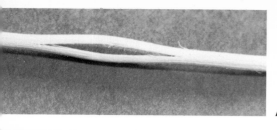

A

B

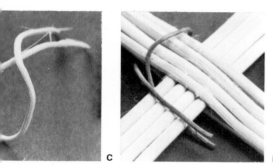

C   D

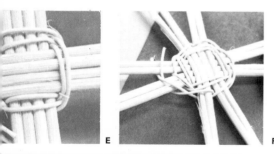

E   F

G

procedure

While natural plant reed is exciting as material for weaving, commercial reed is usually more easily available and may be purchased in the form of round or flat strands of various diameters and widths. Commercial reed often comes in skeins and is usually dry and brittle, but soaking in water for a short time will make it pliable for cutting and manipulating. When used for handles or spokes, reed can be cut to specific lengths before soaking. To prepare for soaking, roll the reed into a loose coil and fasten its end by twisting. Since reed is most pliable while damp, wrap it in soft material such as terry cloth to keep it moist until needed.

It will be helpful to know some basketry techniques when experimenting with reed weaving. First of all, a tight, firm base is essential to the entire form. The reeds of the base, called spokes, lie flat. Some spokes are inserted through slits of other spokes and all radiate from the center. They may be cut to the length needed for the base size, or long enough for weaving the entire form.

ROUND BASE—Using reed made pliable by soaking, select four spokes and cut a slit lengthwise in the middle of each as shown in Photo A. Make these slits large enough so that four additional spokes may be pushed through them. Lay the four spokes closely side by side. Place the four additional spokes, also close together, perpendicular to the first four and push them through the slits in the first four to form a symmetrical cross (Photo B). The weaving proceeds around the center of this four-armed cross.

To begin the weaving, use a thinner reed than that used for spokes and bend it at its mid-point to form a loop around one of the four arms of the cross (Photo C). Fit the reed close to the center of the cross and keep its two loose ends of equal length. Cross these ends and weave them around the second arm of the crosses (Photo D). Cross the ends again and weave them around the third arm. Repeat with the fourth arm and continue to weave the two reed ends around the center of the cross. This is known as the pairing technique (Photo E).

The next step is to separate the spoke of the cross, making them pairs of adjacent reeds. Weave reed-ends over and under these pairs often enough to hold the spokes firmly in place (Photo F). Once more, separate the cross arms, this time making single spokes (Photo G). Weave in and around each individual spoke until the base attains the desired circular shape and size. The base may be strengthened by using larger reed around the edge.

A variation of the simple round base is made by weaving a finish around the edge of the base, continuing to use the same pairing weave. First, decide on the diameter of the base; cut the base spokes at least six inches longer than the diameter. Continue weaving the base as previously described, using the pairing weave for the largest part of the base. When the desired size of base is reached, weave the extra length of the spokes into one another to form a finished edge (Photos H and I).

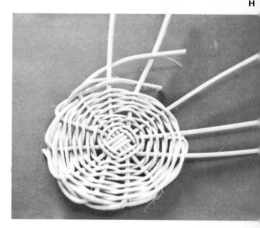

H

I

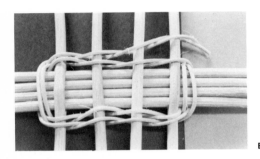

A

B

C

D

THE OVAL BASE—The oval base is a variation of the round base. Decide upon the number of base spokes, then cut half of them to one length and the other half slightly shorter. Cut slits in the centers of the shorter group of spokes. Push the long spokes through these center slits. Space the short spokes some distance apart (Photo A). Begin weaving with the pairing techniques as explained previously. Continue to twist the thin reed around all the side, or shorter spokes, then again around the whole group of spokes, and so on for at least two cycles (Photo B).

Separate the groups of spokes into individual spokes as the weaving proceeds. Continue to pair-weave, pulling the spokes a little farther apart with each row of weaving to produce an oval shape (Photo C). The pairing technique can then be used to finish off the edges.

WOODEN BASE—A wooden base can be of any shape or size. Commercial bases usually come with holes drilled for the reed. However, a wood base may be cut and holes drilled to the size needed for the reeds.

Decide upon the length of reed necessary for constructing the sides. When the reed stands in a vertical position, it is called a stake. The basic stakes are those that fit into the holes and stand perpendicular to the base. Around these, the shape is woven.

To vary the design and give the ends that stick through the bottom a finished appearance, extend the stakes a few inches on the underside. Bend one stake-end down, weaving in and out around the following three stakes (Photo D). Continue this process until all stake-ends are woven in front and back of one another on the underside. Clip off the excess reed.

For variety, extend the basic stakes through the wood bottom and drive wooden beads onto the reed (Photo E). This not only holds the reed securely, but also produces an interesting base. If the beads are loose, because their holes are larger than the reeds, cut additional pieces of reed and stuff into each bead hole. This will hold the bead in place.

SIDES—The sides of the basket are an integral part of the base and rise from it. There are many ways of weaving the sides. After becoming familiar with one method, experiment with others. Begin bending the ends of the base reeds slightly upward. If the original base spokes are too stiff for easy bending, cut them off close to the woven base and insert more pliable reed between the original base spokes. Another method is to insert vertical stakes through the spaces in the woven edging. These verticals provide a structure through which the form is woven. It is important to remember that unless the spokes are damp, they will not bend, and may break.

The next step involves a fairly easy type of weaving which is called waling. Waling is used to strengthen the form as its side takes shape. To do waling weave, use three strands of reed. Place two strands on opposite sides of a vertical stake; cross them and then pass them around the next stake, etc. The third strand is then twined into the previous weave by weaving it over the top of the two crossed strands, then in front of the next two stakes and under the next cross (Photo F).

E

F

Weaving called waling.

Waling combined with open work.

variations

SIDE VARIATIONS—To achieve interest in spacing and accenting designs, use leather strips, wooden balls, bamboo bits, or beads as decorations (Photo A). Combine round and flat reed (Photo B). Vary the size of the round reed and the width of the flat reed (Photo C). Insert extra stakes (Photo D). Place round reed next to flat reed and alternate (Photo E).

EDGES—Whatever form is created, the final edge gives it a finished appearance. Experiment to develop interesting and unusual edges.

D

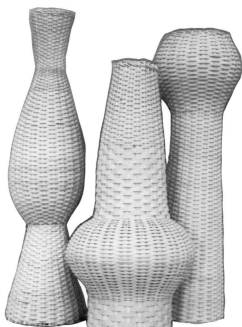

E

Sculptural forms.

Sydel Ackerman, Livingston, N.J.

Indian Basketry

The ancient weaving process of basketry, while highly commercialized today, may still be seen as an art practiced by some Cherokee Indians. Although most Cherokees have adopted the white man's commercial materials and methods, a few retain their traditional techniques and use native materials. The Indian works with a relaxed feeling toward his weaving, carefully planning and shaping each piece. A medium-sized basket may require three days to complete. (See photos of the Cherokee Indian at work.)

The following photos illustrate the working process as the Cherokee Indian makes a basket.

Basket materials prepared for weaving.

Removing rough areas from white oak.

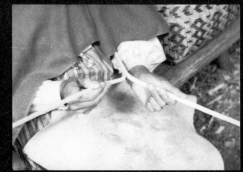
Separating white oak into strips.

Thinning the strips further.

Starting a basket.

Various carved handles prepared for weaving.

The reed is tightened by pushing down on the horizontal reed bands.

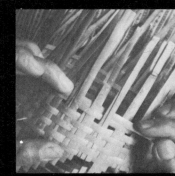
Weaving with river cane.

A completed basket.

OTHER IMAGINATIVE IDEAS & TECHNIQUES

12

Crayoned lines can give the effect of weaving.

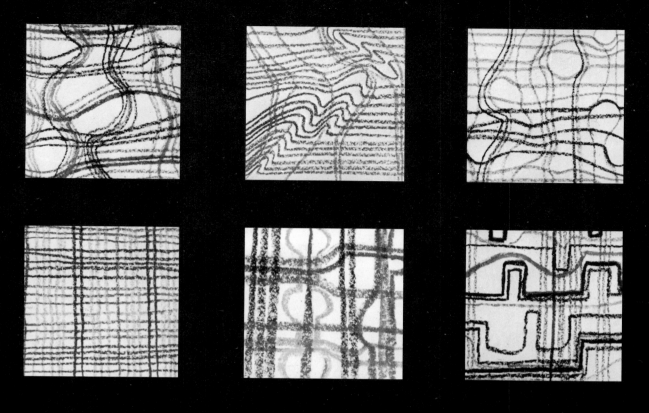

Brayer Printing: A weaving effect emerges when string is wrapped around a linoleum brayer that has been rolled in paint, then onto paper.   The interwoven lines depend upon how the string has been placed on the roller.

weaving with lines

1

Materials from nature: corn husks, fungi, alfalfa, weeds, barley, cattails.

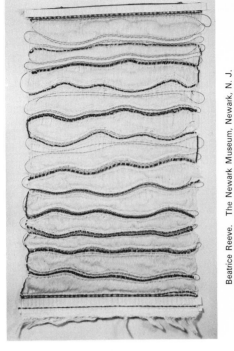

2 *weaving with unlikely materials*

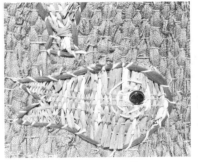

Fabric strips and raffia.

Strips of cotton for weft.

Felt used for warp and weft.

Flat reed used for warp and weft.

Warp and weft made with raffia. Rachel Sullivan, Supervisor of Art, Westfield, New Jersey.

Wheat woven into paper weaving. Grade 1. Courtesy Joan Foucht, Columbus, Ohio.

Yarn Necklace made on piece of cardboard
by Barbara Markey Wallace, New York City.

Pendant by Cheryl Tackett, Ridgefield High School, Conn.

Hairpiece and necklace made of metallic cord and yarn.

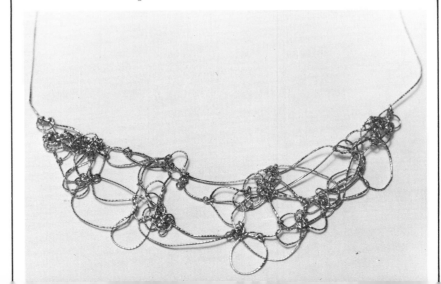

God's eye made of popsicle sticks, courtesy Victoria Bedford Betts.

BASIC MATERIALS
Twigs, branches, ice cream sticks
Scissors
Paste (especially good is rubber cement or tri-tex paste)
Yarn

OPTIONAL MATERIALS
Toothpicks
Lollipop sticks
Bamboo sticks
Wire from coat hangers
Dowel rods
Flat ice-cream or popsicle sticks
Yarns of various kinds including angora and mohair

1

2

3

4

5

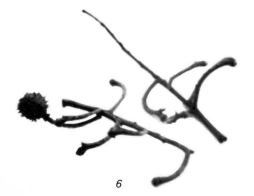

6

1   Front and back of design made on popsicle sticks.

2   Twigs or branches can also be used for the base or beginning of the design.

3   To fasten twigs, paste together or twist wire or rubber band around center. It is also possible to hold the twigs together with yarn.

4   Wrap yarn around two parts of twig, spanning the space between. Avoid crossing strands over one another. Make design on both front and back of shape. Experiment to find ways that work best for you.

5   Continue to span the space between the twigs with strands of yarn. Change colors for more interest.

6   A variation of the god's eye technique is to use a complicated twig or put two twigs together.

variations

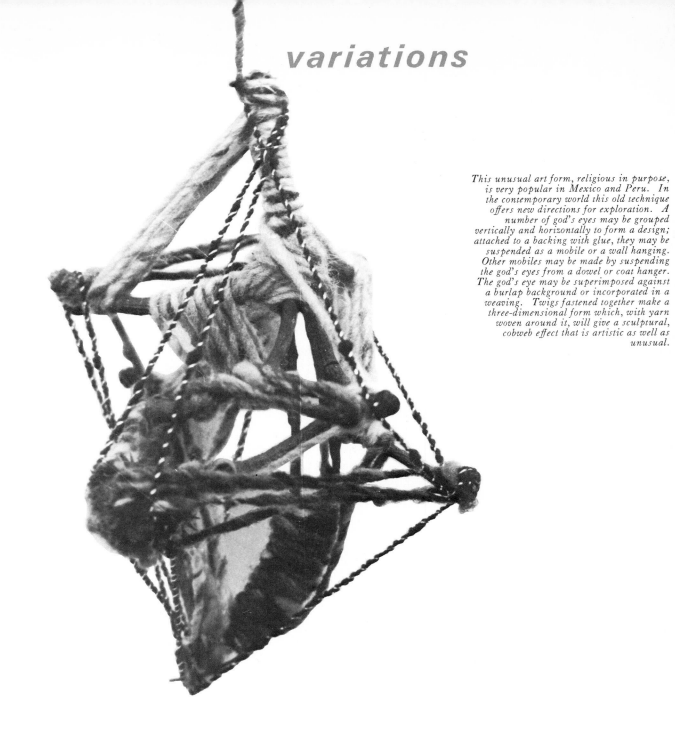

This unusual art form, religious in purpose, is very popular in Mexico and Peru. In the contemporary world this old technique offers new directions for exploration. A number of god's eyes may be grouped vertically and horizontally to form a design; attached to a backing with glue, they may be suspended as a mobile or a wall hanging. Other mobiles may be made by suspending the god's eyes from a dowel or coat hanger. The god's eye may be superimposed against a burlap background or incorporated in a weaving. Twigs fastened together make a three-dimensional form which, with yarn woven around it, will give a sculptural, cobweb effect that is artistic as well as unusual.

variation of needlepoint 5

Scrim, a material discussed in a previous chapter, makes a good background for needlepoint. Customarily needlepoint stitches are made in one direction but, even with a frame, this results in some distortion of the scrim backing. To avoid this distortion, make the stitches in two directions as shown in the rug example. This technique opens new areas of exploration for the designer.

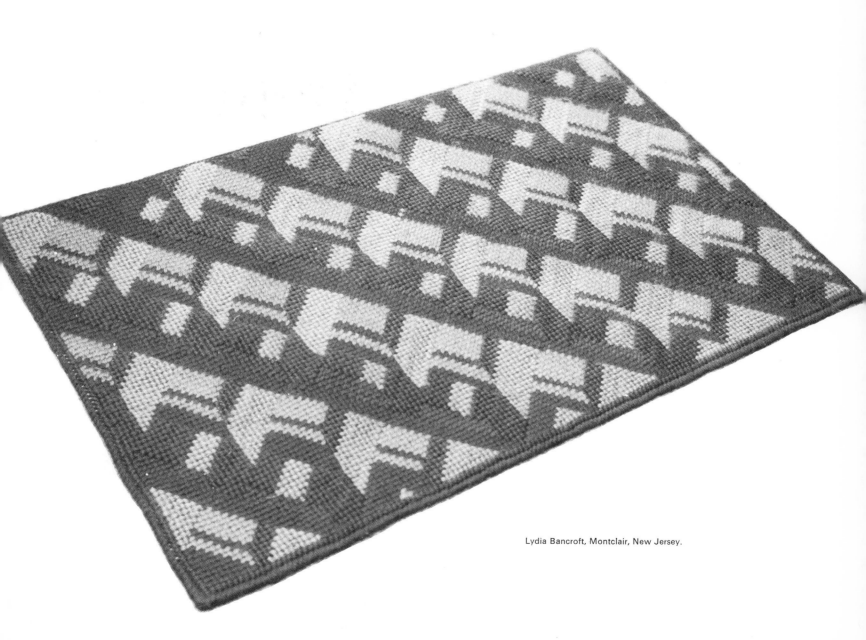

Lydia Bancroft, Montclair, New Jersey.

variation of knitting
6

1. Knot the yarn around the first top left nail.

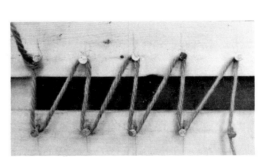

2. Pull the yarn down and around the bottom nail; up, over, and around the second top nail, etc. Continue this winding of yarn until all the nails have been used.

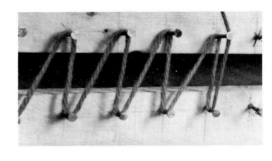

3. Begin to wind the yarn back toward the left end of the slot. As the yarn is wound over the nails, the bottom strand is pulled up, over and off the nail to form a loop.

4. Continue this process for each nail.

With an understanding of this process knitted patterns can be varied by winding the yarn several times around the same nail or different nail combinations.

86

5. As the weaving progresses, the work slips through the opening between the nails in the frame.

13

BASIC MATERIALS
Cardboard or wood frame
String of assorted colors
Wool
Scissors
Straight pins
Weft materials
  Tinsel
  Ribbon
  Fabric
  Yarn
  Nylons
  Tissue paper
  Cellophane
Dowels, small strips of wood or cardboard

OPTIONAL MATERIALS
Assortment of weft supplies
  Leather
  Reed
  Jute
  Rope
Glass and metal rods
Sticks or thin tree branches

tapestry
weaving

The word tapestry awakens visions of splendor and ingeniously woven scenes from a half-forgotten time when medieval artists immortalized with threads the legends, history, and everyday pursuits of their time. Tapestries, particularly in the Middle Ages, were used in parades, at tournaments, and in adornment of the walls of cathedrals and castles. Although an old art, the use of tapestry techniques today can add new interest to simple weaving patterns. There are many adaptations of these techniques which allow for expression of the weaver's ideas.

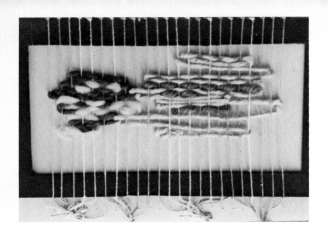

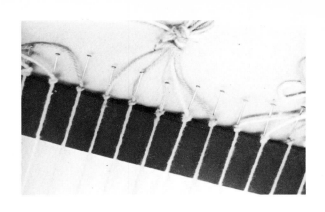

Tapestry techniques are used in several of the weaving methods described in previous chapters. These techniques may be combined with other techniques or employed for the entire weaving. When used for the entire design, cardboard or wood frames make practical devices for holding the warp. PREPARATION OF FRAME: Three methods may be suggested for preparing the frame for weaving. In the first, ordinary straight pins are inserted along the top and bottom edges of the frame; a string is tied around the first end pin of the top row, gently pulled down and wrapped around the first end pin of the bottom row. After tying the string, this procedure is followed for all the pins. In the second method, the string is wrapped around all the pins and tied only to the first and last pin. A third way is to wrap the warp completely around the frame with slits in the cardboard anchoring the warp and keeping the strands vertical. When a wood frame is used, the warp is wrapped tightly so the strands will keep their position without anchoring.

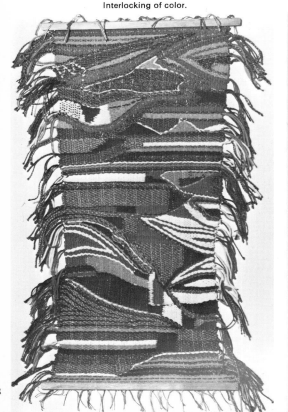

Interlocking of color.

Open areas using slit technique.

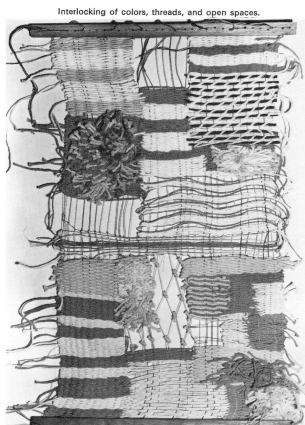

Interlocking of colors, threads, and open spaces.

variations

Techniques which can be combined with tapestry weaving to produce different textural effects.

Elementary/Minneapolis, Minn. Public Schools. Exhibited at American Crayon Co. Studio, New York City. A laid-in tapestry design.

Luis Garrido, Madrid, Spain.

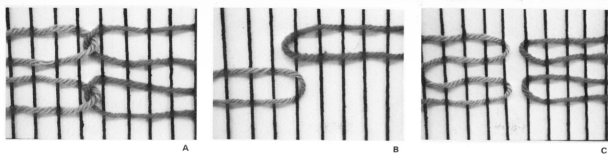

A   B   C

College level.

procedure

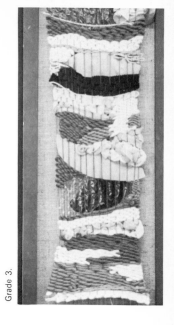

Grade 3.

Tapestry weaving employs the basic technique of linking areas of adjacent weft threads which may be similar or different in color. This is done by interlocking strands of single, double, or even triple threads (Photo A); wrapping weft threads from opposite directions around the same warp thread (Photo B); or weaving part way across the warp and back again, leaving an open area in pattern (Photo C). To make a tapestry design, weave only part way across the warp, reversing the weaving direction of the weft thread at different points of the weaving process.

Many weavers create their tapestry patterns by weaving spontaneously, while others make pre-planned drawings. The weaver who makes a drawing may use it as a guide or reference for weaving a design having one or many shapes. The weaver can draw the shape (animal, person, or bird) in silhouette on a sheet of paper, using crayon or paint to plan the sections of color. Large areas of color work best. After the warp is stretched on a frame or cardboard, the prepared design can be placed under the strands of warp as a guide. It is easier to weave the shape first, then the background. Once the basic procedure is understood, the weaver can explore different approaches to find the one that will serve him best in applying the basic tapestry techniques discussed earlier in the chapter.

Elementary, Minneapolis, Minn. Public Schools. Exhibited at American Crayon Co. Studio, New York City.

Detail of wall hanging/College Student.

Detail/Tapestry technique with shells and pipe cleaners interwoven into the pattern. Piece is mounted on wood as a wall hanging.

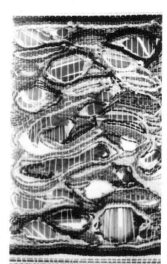

Colored celluloid woven into warp as accent. The warp is held by glass rods at top and bottom.

91

Courtesy Samie Anderson, Teacher, Montclair Public Schools, New Jersey, Grade 2.

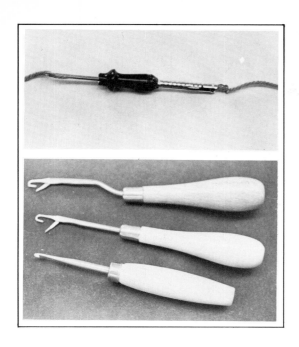

BASIC MATERIALS

Rugs with burlap backing

Burlap or 2-ply monk's cloth

Rug hook or Columbia Minerva punch

Needle

Yarn

Frame

Staple

Wrapping paper

Crayon or Felt tip marker

Rugs with scrim backing

Scrim (sometimes called rug canvas)

Yarn

Frame

Stapler

Loop latch hooker

Wrapping paper

Felt tip marker

Courtesy Ed Chandless, Hanover, N.J.

rug hooking

The technique of rug hooking, which is simple enough for children, employs the use of a tool with a hooked end to pull and push yarn back and forth through a background material. It is effective when combined with weaving or stitchery; like weaving, it can stimulate the weaver to experience the excitement of working with smooth, rough, hard and soft yarns. Designing new and varied arrangements of color, texture, and pattern will challenge the ingenuity. Ranging from shag effects to low relief sculpture, this art may take the form of inviting rugs for floor or wall hangings.

Ideas for design are everywhere: a painting or print, cut paper shapes, plant life viewed through a microscope, shapes of buildings, nature—all the endless visual patterns in our daily lives offer constant and changing sources.

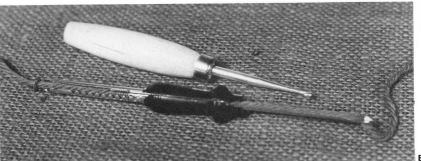

A

B

procedure

Two basic rug hooking procedures may be used as a beginning for making any rug or wall hanging. These procedures form the basis from which the designer can branch out to find his own approach through experimentation. The first method involves the use of a backing fabric of burlap or monk's cloth and any one of three tools: the punch needle, shuttle hooker, or hand hook (with a crochet needle as a possible substitute for the last). The second method makes use of a tool called the loop latch hook and a backing material of scrim.

To use the punch needle and burlap in the first method, decide on the rug size; then cut burlap for a backing, allowing several extra inches on each edge for a margin. Use a handmade frame of soft wood, a ready-made picture frame, or one of the specially designed stretcher or rug frames. Stretch the backing tightly over the frame and fasten with staples or carpet tacks. Cut a piece of wrapping paper the size of the proposed rug. With crayon, felt tip pen, or chalk, draw a bold design that will fill the space inside the margin (Photo A). Avoid tiny detail and line drawings.

To transfer the design, sketch directly on the burlap with a felt pen or charcoal; paint a design on the burlap with dye; or cut out the shape and use it as a pattern.

To use the punch needle, thread the yarn through ring at top of the handle and then through the inside point. Pull about a foot of yarn through the needle; then drag the yarn back, with tension, so it will gradually slip into the tube and handle. Set the loop gauge for the length of loop wanted (Photo B). Point the open side of the punch needle in the direction the hooking will take (Photo C). Push the needle through the backing until it hits the handle, keeping the hand firmly on the burlap (Photo D). Pull the needle back to the surface (Photo E). Do not jerk, but glide it from one loop to another. Continue the process of punching the needle back and forth through the burlap (Photo F). When a small amount of hooking has been completed, the loops will begin to hold one another tightly (Photo G).

C D E F G

George Wells hooking a rug

Courtesy George Wells, "The Ruggery", Glen Head, L.I.

A

B

C

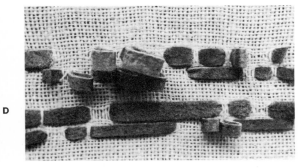

D

The hooking technique makes a surface that has both visual and tactile appeal. A variety of textures result from snipping the end of each loop to give a velvety appearance (Photo A); shearing the tops off the loops (Photo B); sculpturing the loops, giving a low-relief effect; varying the length of loops, making some high and others low (Photo C); combining clipped and unclipped loops; or combining yarn, strips of fabric or leather (Photo D).

When all parts of the design are finished, remove the rug from the frame, then fold back the edges and stitch (Photo E). Paint latex sizing over the back of the finished piece to give body to the rug, hold the yarn securely in place, and prevent slipping on the floor. If the rug is to be a wall hanging, sizing will not be necessary.

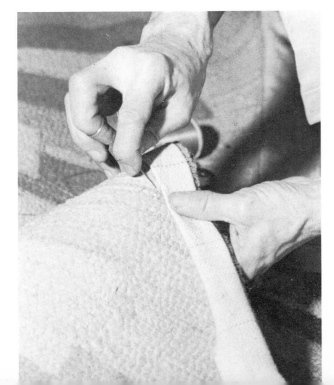

E

George Wells finishes edges of rug by folding back extra material for a margin. He tacks it down by stitching.

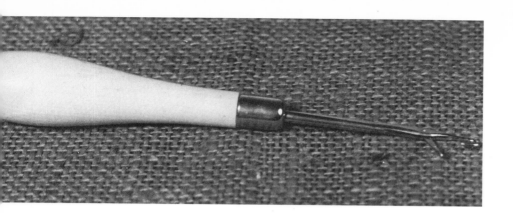

SCRIM BACKGROUND

The loop latch hook, used when working with a scrim backing, knots the yarn into the backing. For this type of rug hooking, cut a piece of scrim, leaving enough material on all four sides to turn back for a finished edge. With a crayon, draw a design on paper to match the size of the rug. Place the paper under the scrim, and with a felt tip pen trace the lines of the design on the material. This procedure is illustrated in the chapter, "Weaving on Scrim." Because of its stiffness, it does not need to be placed on a frame.

Cut pieces of yarn the length desired, usually about two inches. To avoid interrupting the hooking process for constant cutting and measuring, prepare enough pieces at one time to complete a small section. Bring the two ends of yarn together and hold between the fingers to form a loose loop. Put the hooker through the loop and under one strand of the scrim. Pull the two ends of the yarn up to the point of the hook and place them between the hook and latch. Close the latch and pull the hooker back through the scrim and also through the previous loop, holding the ends of yarn with fingers to form a knot in the yarn. Continue this process, keeping the loops close together.

This simple introduction to hooking techniques has merely scratched the surface of the wide range of possibilities suggested by this medium. Experiment and discover new avenues, new methods and new combinations.

variation

An unusual variation to the hooking technique is rug hooking at the easel. A large piece of scrim is attached to a wood frame, then placed on an easel, which serves only to hold the frame. Several weavers can work simultaneously as each makes his design for a particular area of the piece. This group approach to rug hooking enables each weaver to see his design emerge, as each shape becomes a part of the finished piece.

the GHIORDEZ knot

A versatile knot that may be combined with weaving or knotted to a coarsely woven backing material.

rug knotting

Detail of knot using cardboard or frame weaving.

Ghiordez knot may also be combined with tabby weaving to make rya rugs. Several rows of tabby may separate each row of knots.

Ghiordez knot

Beginning of loop.

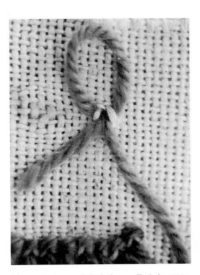

View of loop as it is being pulled down to form a knot.

Yarn has been pulled tight to form a knot. As a new knot is started, a loop is left at the bottom. The entire design may be made with cut or uncut loops. To make loops of equal size, place the yarn strand under a horizontal rod before entering the background material. This will serve as a gauge for loop lengths.

PROVOCATIVE VARIATIONS

which the weaver may explore

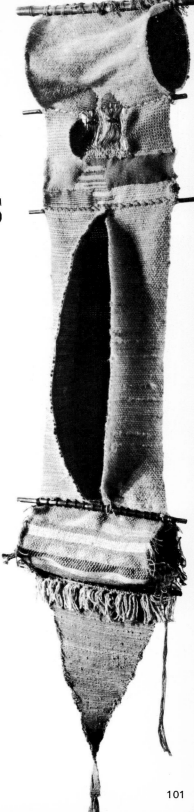

Dorian Zachai, Photo Courtesy
American Craftsmen's Council.

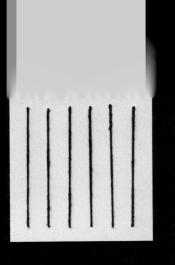    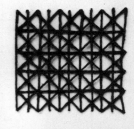

15

1. Using wooden frame or notched cardboard, stretch warp threads vertically from top to bottom.

2. Stretch threads horizontally.

3. Stretch threads at slant from top left to bottom right.

4. Slant threads top right to bottom left.

5. Stretch a second set of vertical strands over the horizontal and slanted strands and in between the first set of vertical strands.

6. With a needle, weave under the intersection of each "X" shaped figure; then make a stitch by looping back over the same. Continue, making a stitch around each "X" shaped intersection. On alternate rows, weave over and under, but do not loop.

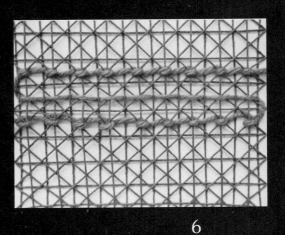

6

Linda Panitz Costello

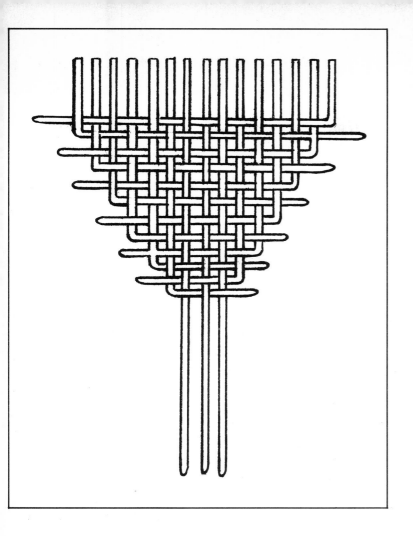

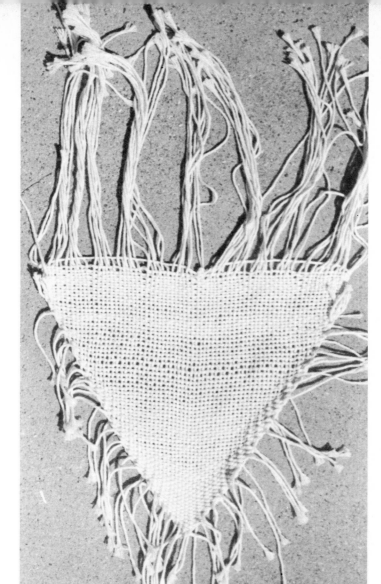

A WOVEN TRIANGLE

The simple woven triangle is an example of how the warp threads may also be used for weft threads. The outside warp thread of one edge is woven under and over the remaining warp. The outside thread of the opposite side is then used for weaving. As the warp threads are decreased in number, the weft threads are increased. This process is repeated until all warp threads have been woven as weft, resulting in a triangle.

103

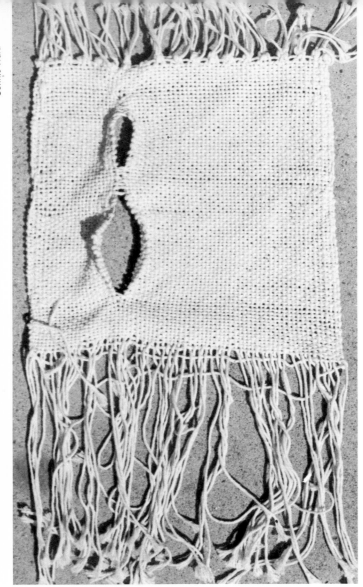

Connie Ward

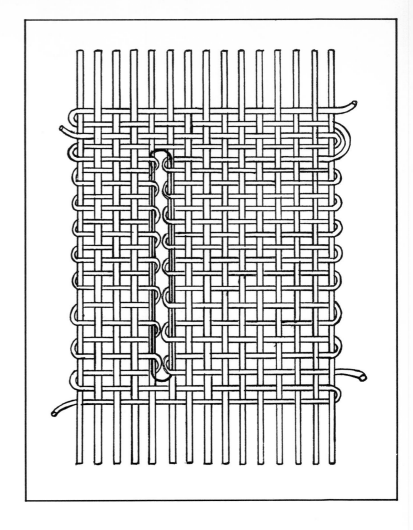

THE SLIT: While the slit is a traditional technique, it can offer an added dimension to the weaving process. One way to make the slit is to fasten a wire to any two warp threads which may later form the slit; then complete the weaving and bend the wire into a pleasing shape. Another method is to allow for the slit as the weaving progresses, then weave a piece of wire through the threads around the edge of the slit.

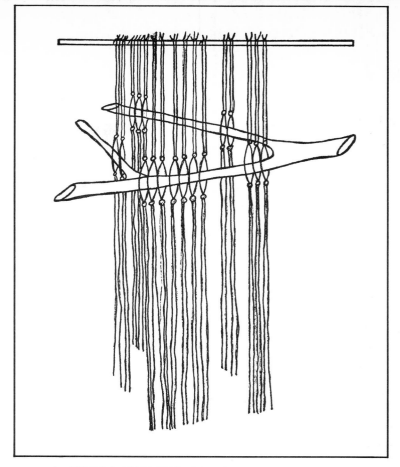

A FORM WOVEN ON A BRANCH

A creative weaver can see possibilities in the simplest devices. Even the tree branch, used by primitive man because he was so limited, can inspire the imaginative person to new and exciting techniques. For this technique, knot two warp strands together at one end and place one strand on each side of the branch; then bring the two threads together and knot. This keeps the warp in the proper position on the branch. Continue fastening the warp in strands of two around the branch until there is enough for weaving. Suspend the branch to permit the warp threads to hang freely for the weaving process. Attach weights to the bottom ends of the warp, thereby providing greater tension. In the example shown here, the warp is arranged so that a cylinder is first formed. Then by gradually eliminating warp threads by weaving them as weft, a conical shape is made.

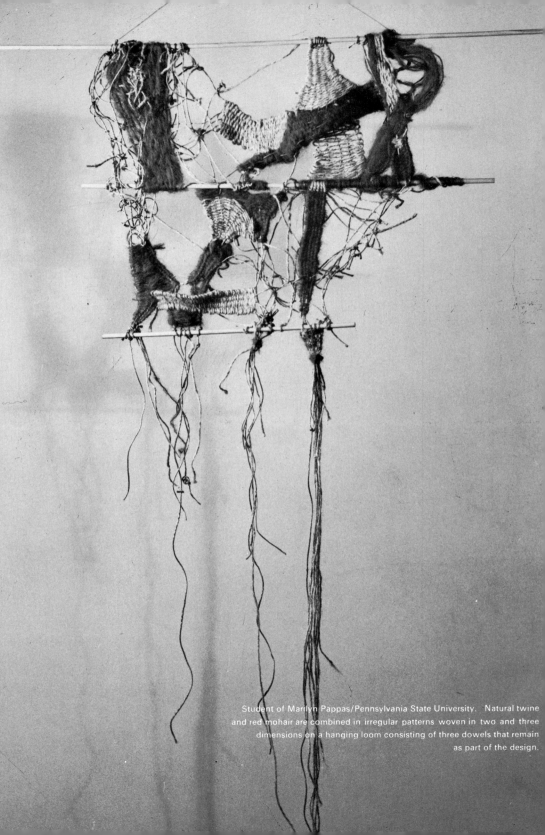

Student of Marilyn Pappas/Pennsylvania State University.   Natural twine
and red mohair are combined in irregular patterns woven in two and three
dimensions on a hanging loom consisting of three dowels that remain
as part of the design.

Free form mobile
made of reed,
gauze impregnated
with plaster,
and yarn.
Gale Youngworth

what

STUDENTS- &

CLASSROOM

TEACHERS

say about weaving

16

WHAT STUDENTS, TEACHERS AND
ARTISTS SAY ABOUT WEAVING
*"Weaving is especially fun because I can feel the
colors instead of just seeing them."*

GLEN HEALEY/First Grade

STUDENTS

"I find the challenge of weaving lies in manipulating color and texture into exciting pattern and form."

LINDA ELY/High School Senior

"I had no specific design in mind; I experimented with ways of weaving over and under threads. My weaving was made on a crude rectangular wood frame with nails hammered along the top and bottom."

RAYE-ELLEN MILLER/College Student

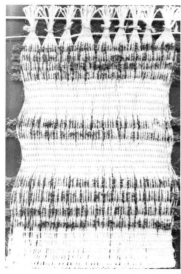

"To begin my weaving, I constructed a simple wood frame and placed finishing nails at top and bottom, one-fourth inch apart. Since I wanted to compose a coarse mat, I chose rough fibrous cords for warp. Rough and smooth materials were selected for weft, including nylon and strips of carpet. The carpet also added strong horizontal lines to the design. Warp cords were bunched in groups and tied. A dowel was later inserted through the cords."

BARRY WITTE/College Student

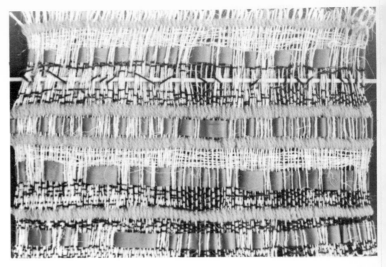

"I find weaving a challenge through which I can find self-expression by expanding traditional techniques into new variations and discovering interesting uses of common materials."

NINA ORSINI/College Student

"I am able to express myself through experimental weaving an find it a more creative method for my purposes than the mechanica loom. My weaving was executed as follows: I fastened two strip of wood to the top and bottom of a sheet of plywood. Finishin nails were hammered part way into the strips. Binder's twin was wound around the nails and stretched from top to bottom serve as warp. Wool yarn and strips of leather were interwove for the weft."

JAY EDWARD FLUCKER/College Studen

CLASSROOM TEACHERS

"*The techniques used in weaving are fairly simple, but they do require and instill an intellectual discipline. On the other hand, the student is free to choose a specific material, design, or technique. This encourages originality and self-expression.*"

FRANCINE DECOTIIS,/Fourth Grade Teacher

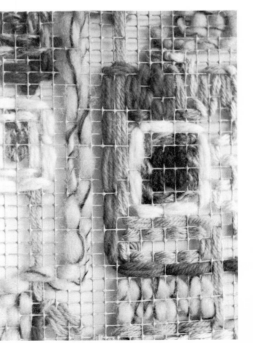

Weaving into wire mesh by fourth grade student.

A pattern was made to plan the design.

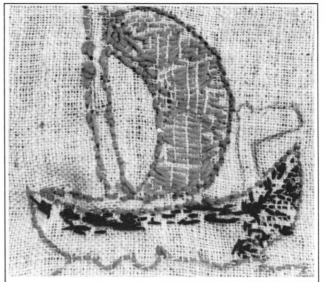

"*A teacher should try to stimulate the creative energies of the student. At the same time she should stress the importance of organization. In my opinion, both of these goals are ideally combined when the child is taught to weave.*"

CLARE GLUTTING/First Grade Teacher

My children find great happiness in weaving. It points them toward constructive self-realization. In addition, it helps the shy student to gain confidence. In this respect, weaving is invaluable. Children must be taught to think through what they intend to do, to visualize some kind of outcome. The teacher must help the child, through guidance, to consider the best way to use his materials, to organize his thoughts and to look ahead to avoid haphazard designing."

ANNA VON BONIN/Sixth Grade Teacher

111

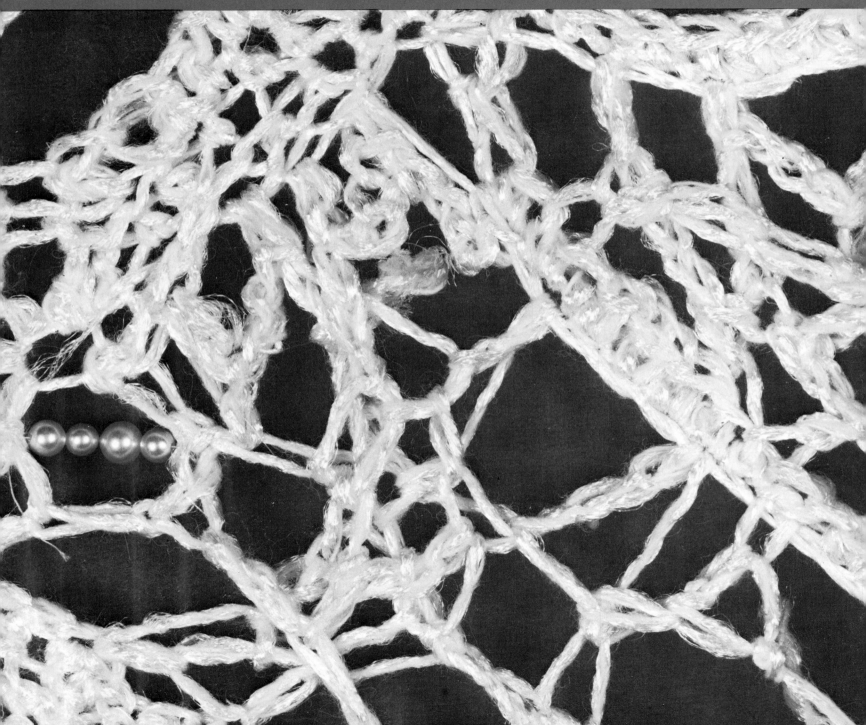

Stitchery superimposed on weaving.

Burlap superimposed on burlap.

Mohair yarn knotted and looped.

Rug hooking with snipped loops.

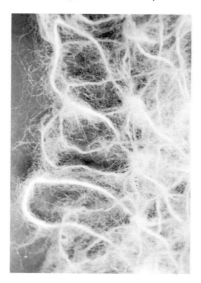

ail of a wall panel made by author
g crochet stitches to create an
rwoven thread pattern.

texture formed by fuzzy materials

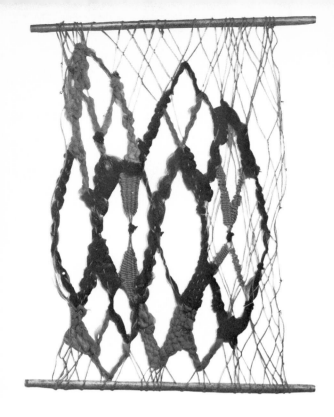

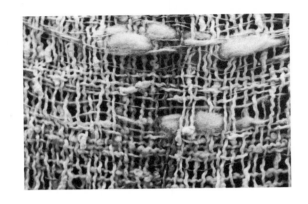

texture formed by open spaces

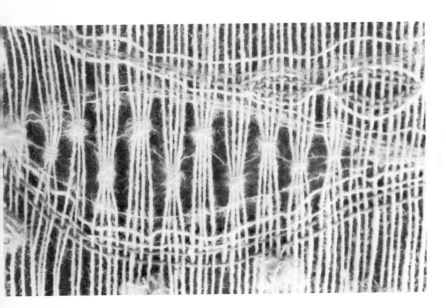

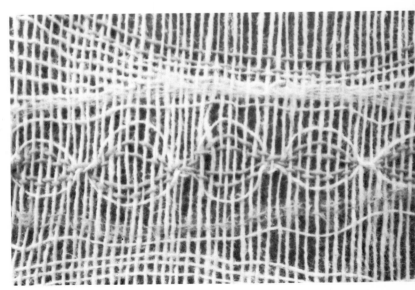

  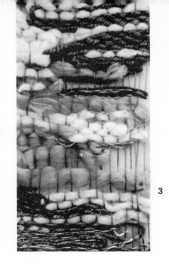 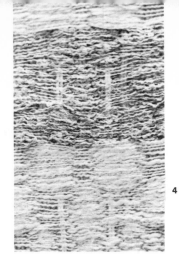 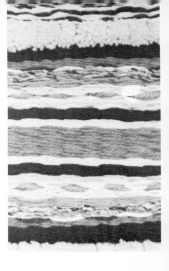

texture formed by materials

1. Yarn woven over cellophane background.
2. Shells and pipe cleaners woven into warp.
3. Nylon hose combined with yarn.
4. Silk nubby threads used for warp.
5. Pieces of carpet used for weft.
6. Jute and mohair combined into design.
7. Tissue paper and yarn used for warp.
8. Twine, string, glass rods, and knots combined.
9. Tongue depressors and ribbon
10. Bamboo strips and yarn.

(9, 10 Courtesy John Nerreau, Supervisor of Art, Bridgeport, Conn.)

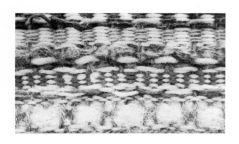  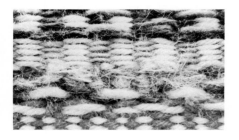

texture formed by woven patterns on cardboard

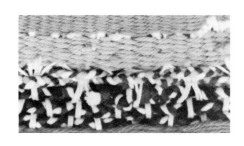

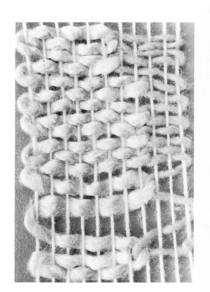

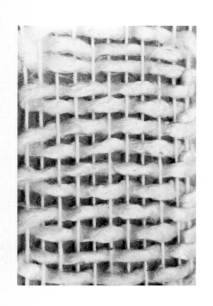 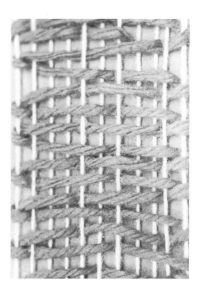 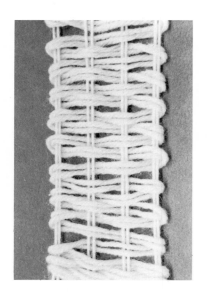

Textures and Weaves.   Claire Zeisler, Chicago, Illinois.

Lace Work, Luba Krejci, Czechoslovakia; Dene Ulin, Agent.

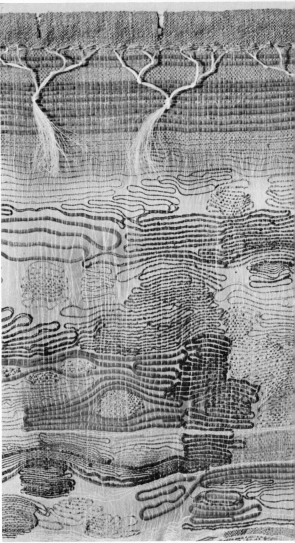

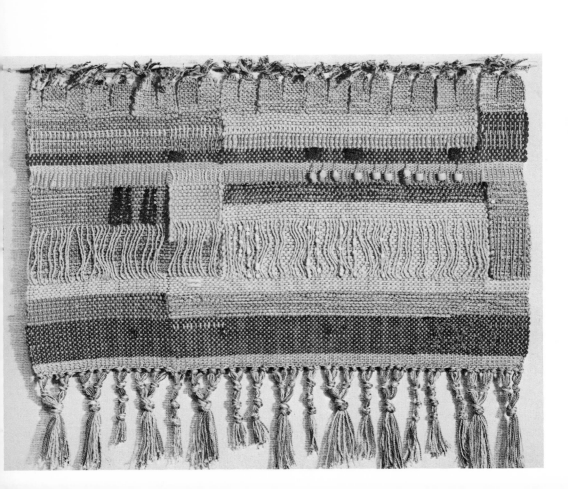

Textures and Weaves. Diane Wiersba,
Charleston, West Va.

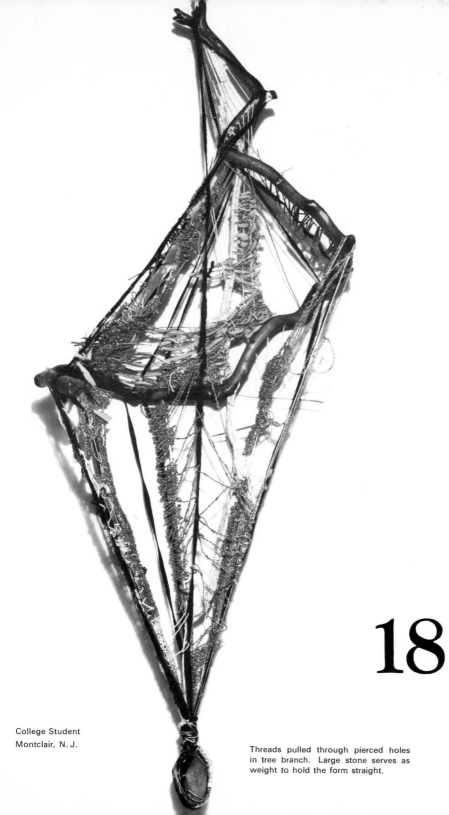

Marilyn R. Pappas, Miami-Dade Jr. College, Florida.

18 *WOVEN FORMS*

College Student
Montclair, N. J.

Threads pulled through pierced holes
in tree branch. Large stone serves as
weight to hold the form straight.

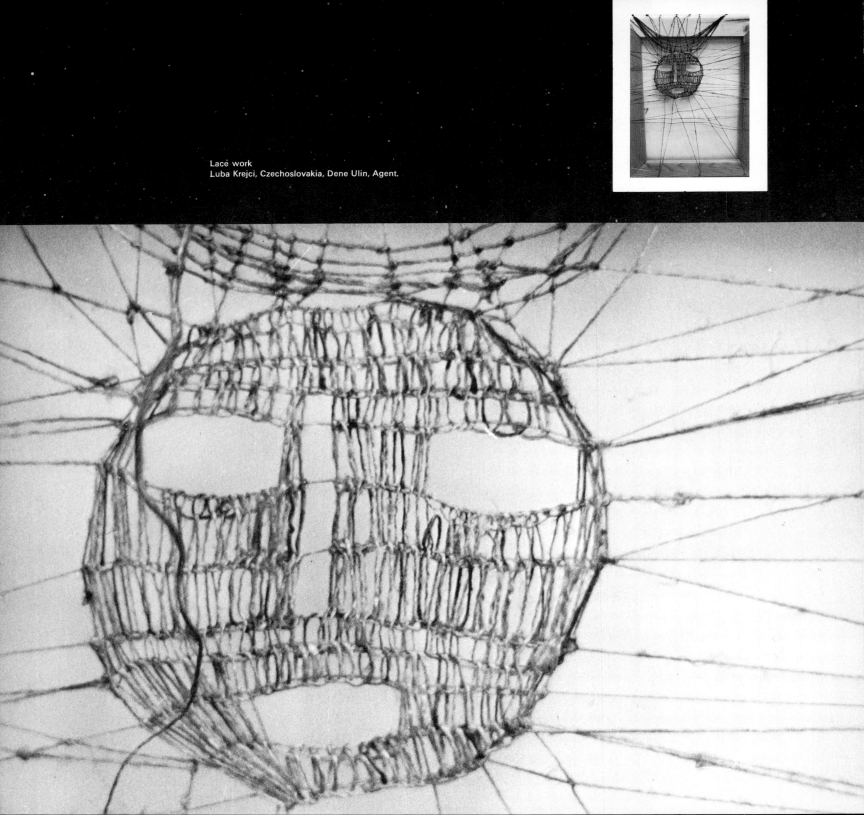

Lace work
Luba Krejci, Czechoslovakia, Dene Ulin, Agent.

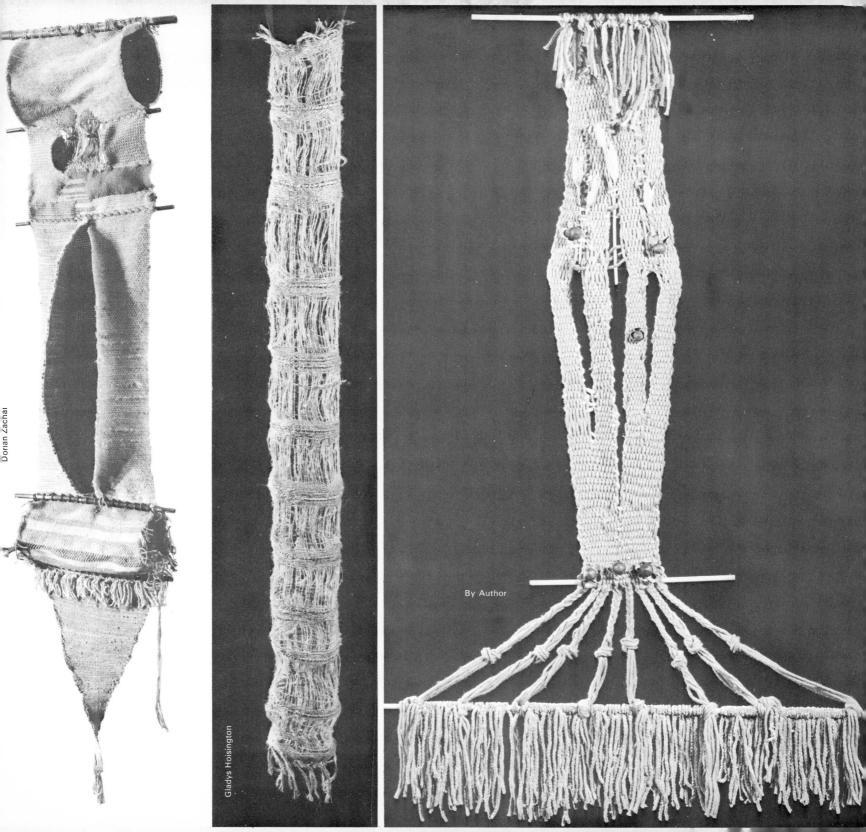

Dorian Zachai

Gladys Hoisington

By Author

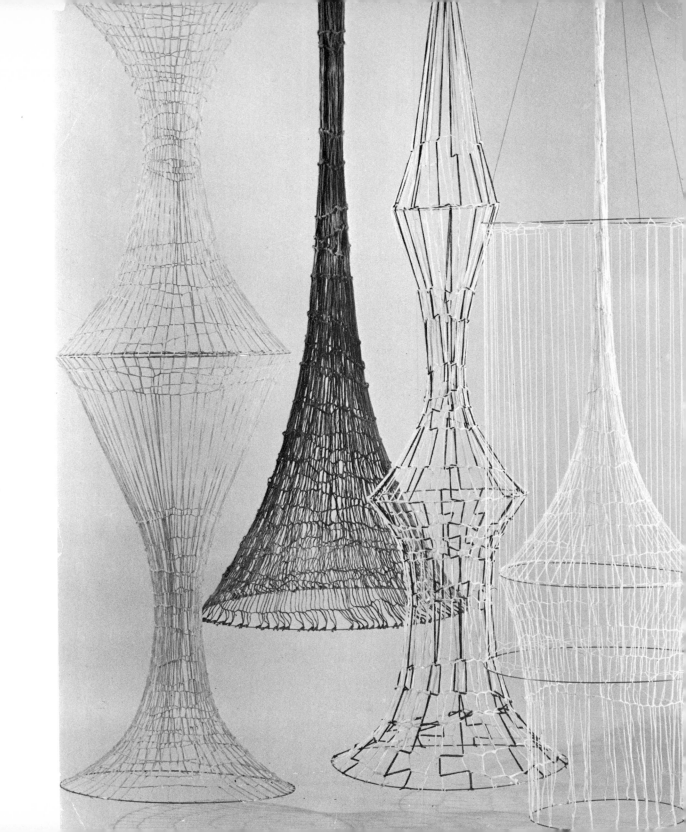

Ted Hallman
Souderton, Pa.

124

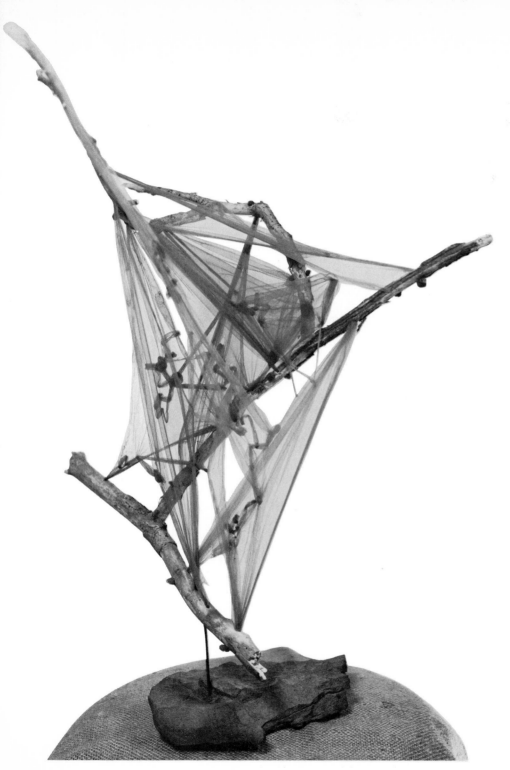

Nylon hose stretched and woven over and around a tree branch, Carol Higbee.

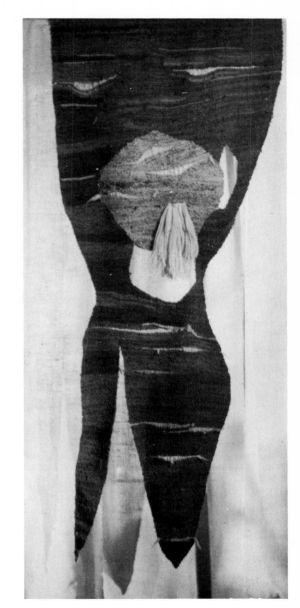

Barbara Shawcroft.

125

GUIDE FOR MATERIALS AND TECHNIQUES

This chart suggests a wide variety of ways the weaver can create designs as he experiments and explores the process of weaving. Refer to the material or technique you plan to employ, then read across the chart (*from left to right*) to find ways in which that material may be used in weaving.

MATERIAL OR TECHNIQUE	COLOR	TEXTURE	SPACE	LINE	SHAPE
PAPER	USE COLOR TO DRAMATIZE: Shades and tints of color. Subdued colors. Contrasting colors such as yellow and dark blue. Warm colors such as red, yellow, orange. Cool colors such as blue or green. Contrasting of warm and cool colors.	Use rough and smooth papers. Use surface enrichments such as paper sculpture and printing techniques.	Use different widths of paper strips. Cut pieces out of paper strips to change spacing.	Cut straight, curved, or jagged slits into a sheet of paper, and weave through them. Cut paper strips in different widths and shapes to use for weaving.	Weave a single shape, then weave around it with a contrasting color. Weave different sized shapes making them large, medium and small. Use related shapes, similar but not identical in appearance.
SCRIM		Use background as part of design. Employ rug hooking techniques for texture. Weave knotted string or yarns into the fabric.	Use the mesh as part of the design, leaving space around woven areas. Cut out parts of the mesh, thereby combining open and solid areas.	Show direction of line by letting it wander over fabric as the line is woven over and under background threads. Show variation in width of line by weaving many rows of threads for a wide line and fewer rows for a thin line.	Make some shapes appear to overlap. Make a design that has different sized shapes over and under entire weaving. Form shapes by making areas of color of different sizes.
MESH					
BURLAP		Pull strands out of the fabric to create open spaces. Use stitchery to give texture.	Pull threads in loosely woven fabrics such as burlap. Tie some threads together to create new space relationships.		
WIRE			Leave some exposed areas of wire.	Use thick and thin yarns to vary width of line. Make curved or angular lines.	
PENCIL		Use fuzzy and hard yarns. Weave with various materials such as nylon stockings, leather strips, pipe cleaners.	Use color to give appearance of space.	Use tapestry techniques to give interest.	Use many warp strands to make wide forms.
STRAWS		Use small pieces of drinking straws as part of design.			Sew shapes together.

COLOR	TEXTURE	SPACE	LINE	SHAPE	
For reed weaving, use reed of natural color or dye with natural or synthetic dyes. Combine reed with other materials such as beads, grasses, sticks, or yarns, to give color. When using the tapestry technique, connect areas of color. Use several strands of different colors, weaving them in combinations. Dye yarns or strips of wool to get more gradations of color. Let color suggest ideas or shapes.	Add stitchery to top surface of weaving. Use a variety of materials in the weaving: cord, string, reed, plastic bags, thin dowel rods, grasses, sticks, beads, glass rods. Weave into previously woven areas. Use different techniques such as tabby, tapestry, soumak. Combine fibers of various textures.	Tie several warp threads together to create interesting space arrangements.	Permit some fibers to function as line and wander throughout the warp. Vary thickness of yarn. Make threads form curved, angular and jagged lines.	Use a heavyweight fiber to make design and a thinner weight to surround the shape. Leave some warp unwoven to serve as open space for part of the design; combine with solidly woven areas.	CARDBOARD FRAME
	Weave with different thicknesses and widths of reed.	Use different width reed. Combine weaving techniques that will create space.	Weave the reed in the directions necessary to make forms; the reed itself acts as line. Vary the width of lines by using different widths of reed.	Let the reed suggest form as it is shaped upward from the base.	REED
	Use different types of threads, yarns, cords, ribbons or strips of fabric to give texture.	Use tapestry techniques to make interesting space.	Use interlocking threads. Inlay threads. Let threads wander through the weaving.	Let a painting inspire ideas for shape. Inlay a central shape. Inlay a group of shapes.	TAPESTRY
	Use loops of different lengths. Snip loops to give a fluffy effect. Sculpture the long loops. Use yarns of different texture or color to give illusion of texture.	Hook areas of color unequal in width and length, or even in different sized shapes.	Use line to give accent or direction in design. Vary the direction and width of line.	Hook areas of color or texture to form shapes. Use color to emphasize important shapes. Use line to accent shape.	RUG HOOKING

MATERIALS

SUPPLIES

Many yarns, needles, wire, and loosely woven fabrics can be purchased in local stores such as department stores, knitting and fabric shops. Hardware cloth and other types of wire screens are available at hardware stores. School supply dealers are another excellent source for a wide variety of weaving materials. In addition, you may purchase by mail order from the following:

1   **Bloomfield Woolen Co.**
Bloomfield, Indiana 47424   *Woolen fabrics in pieces or strips*

2   **Bon Bazar Ltd.**
149 Waverly Place
New York, N.Y. 10014   *Burlap in assorted colors*

3   **Borgs of Lund**
Box 96
Lund, Sweden   *Variety of yarns, including rya and flossa yarns*

4   **The Burnhams**
1305 Del Valle
La Puente, California 91744   *Scotland Wool*

5   **Charles Y. Butterworth**
2222 E. Susquehanna Ave.
Philadelphia, Pennsylvania 19125   *Yarns, linen, wool, cotton, loop, rayon, novelty, ratine*

6   **W. Cushing and Co.**
Dover-Foxcroft
Maine 04426   *Dyes—94 shades*

7   **Contessa Yarns**
Dept. H. W.
P. O. Box 37
Lebanon, Connecticut 06249   *Various assorted colors of yarns Also natural yarns available for home dyeing*

8   **Wm. Condon & Sons**
65 Queen St., P.O. Box 129
Charlottetown, P. E. Island, Can.   *Weaving yarns suitable for blankets, rugs and upholstery*

9   **The Countryside Handweavers**
Box 1225
Mission, Kansas 66222   *Swiss Linen Yarns*

10   **Fair-Tex Distributing Co.**
868 Sixth Ave.
New York, New York 10001   *Odd lots in jumbo and small surprise packages and linens*

11   **Frederick J. Fawcett, Inc.**
129 South St.
Boston, Massachusetts 02111   *Imported linen yarns*

12   **D. Jay Products, Inc.**
P. O. Box 797
Newark, New Jersey 07101   *Novelty threads and chenille stems*

13 House of Kleen
P. O. Box 58
Essex, Connecticut 06426

Yarns from Sweden

14 Lily Mills Co.
Shelby, North Carolina 28150

Wide selection of cotton, wool, metallic, rayon yarns
Embroidery threads of all kinds

15 Paternayan Bros., Inc.
312 East 95th St.
New York, New York 10028

Large variety of yarns—crewel, tapestry and knitting "Duraback" and monk's cloth for rug hooking

16 Rug Design Studio
Black Mountain, North
Carolina 28711

Rug canvas and yarn

17 The Ruggery
Cedar Swamp Rd.
Glen Head, L. I., N.Y. 11545

Rug hooking supplies, yarns, monk's cloth

18 Shuttlecraft
P.O. Box 6041
Providence, Rhode Island
02904

Imported Linen Yarns

19 Tranquillity Studio
West Cornwall, Connecticut
06796

American outlet for Briggs and Little yarns. Specialty in black sheep yarn

20 Troy Yarn and Textile Co.
603 Mineral Spring Ave.
Pawtucket, Rhode Island
02860

A wide variety of yarns
Special rug yarns

21 J. C. Yarn Co.
109-111 Spring St.
New York, New York 10012

Yarns

22 Yarn Depot, Inc.
545 Sutter St., Dept. 1
San Francisco, California
94102

Handspun wools
Single ply white sheep. Very irregula and lumpy

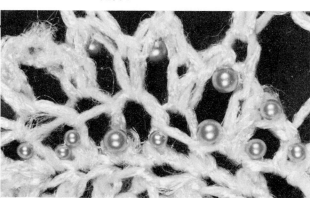

Detail, lace construction by author.

GLOSSARY

Bye-Spokes—Extra spokes inserted beside the first spokes to strengthen the weaving.

Canvas Stretcher—Strips of wood fitted together to form a frame. Small triangles are inserted at corners to make frame sturdy.

Collage—A design or picture made by pasting an arrangement of materials on a background.

Cross-Stitch Canvas—A coarse, starched-like cloth usually woven in a regular mesh. May be used for tapestry, embroidery or rug hooking. Sometimes called scrim.

Dowel Rods—Wooden rods used for hanging finished work. They may be inserted through the warp threads of the weaving, or the top of the weaving may be lapped over the rod.

Felt-Tip Pens—Tube-like markers with felt tips, available in assorted colors.

God's Eye—A small cross, often made of twigs or branches, with colored yarn or thread wound around in the shape of a square set in a diagonal position.

Latch Loop Hook—A tool with a hook and latch at one end, set in a wooden handle.

Latex Sizing—A liquid rubber used for painting the back of a hooked rug.

Low-Relief—Projections at intermediate levels.

Mono-Print—One print, made by creating a design with water soluble paint on a surface, then placing a fabric flat on top of the design. By rubbing over the fabric, the design is transferred to cloth. The cloth is then lifted from the paint and dried.

Pairing—Using two reeds at the same time, twisting with each reed alternately.

Potato Print—A print made by cutting a potato in half and carving a design into the flat surface. When ink or paint is applied to the design, it may be printed on cloth or paper.

Punch Needle—A tool with a gauge for setting length of loop. Used for hooking technique.

Randing—In basketry, the over-and-under weave, in front of one stake and behind the next, with a single reed. It is best to have an uneven number of stakes for this weave.

Rug Hook—Similar to a crochet hook set in a wood handle; used for rug hooking

Scrim—A fabric often used as backing for rug hooking. Sometimes called cross-stitch canvas.

Spokes—Reeds that radiate from the center of the base of a basket form.

Stakes—The upright reeds which form the foundation upon which the basket sides are woven.

Stitchery—Various types of stitches combined to form a design.

Structural Skeleton—The arrangement of warp threads.

Tabby—A simple pattern developed by weaving over and under alternate threads.

Tapestry—A type of over-and-under weaving, employing the basic tapestry technique of linking adjacent weft threads which may be similar or different in color.

Taut—Tightly drawn threads or fabric.

Waling—The use of three strands of reed woven in a twined effect.

Warp—A series of threads that lie in a vertical position.

Weft—Horizontal threads or fibers used for weaving over-and-under the warp.

The author often uses a picture frame for weaving. This illustration shows one of her panels woven with yarn and twigs. As a professional weaver, she feels this method offers unlimited possibilities to create in both two and three dimensions.

*T*HE *creative and perceptive approach demonstrated in this book shows only one aspect of Sarita Rainey's varied career as teacher, artist and craftsman. As Art Supervisor for the Montclair, New Jersey Public Schools, she is deeply involved in the daily challenge of art education. She brings to weaving a talent and versatility that have found expression in her enameling, silver work and oil painting.*

In this book Miss Rainey presents the simple and imaginative weaving techniques she has developed through her exploration of weaving as a designer-craftsman. As you will see, the results are exciting and colorful. Miss Rainey received her B.S. from Kent State University of Ohio and was awarded graduate degrees in Fine Arts and Art Education by Teachers College, Columbia University. She has been guest lecturer in Design at the University of British Columbia, Vancouver, and on the faculty of Paterson State College, New Jersey. Her work has been widely exhibited at such places as the Smithsonian Institution, New York World's Fair, and the Contemporary Crafts Museum. Miss Rainey is a member of the executive board of the New Jersey Designer-Craftsmen. Underlying these many activities is her main goal, so well illustrated by this book: to help teachers expand the imagination and expressive capacity of students for a deeper, more sensitive and satisfying understanding of the world around them.

The Publisher

BIBLIOGRAPHY

Allbon, Leonard G.
Basic Basketry
Altrincham, Great Britain
The St. Ann's Press, 1961

Black, Mary E.
New Key to Weaving
Milwaukee
Bruce Publishing Co., 1957

Carrel, Alexis
Man, the Unknown
New York
Harper & Row, Publishers, Inc., 1939

Christopher, F. J.
Basketry (edited by Marjorie O'Shaughnessy)
New York
Dover Publications, Inc., 1952

Gallinger, Osma Couch and Benson, Oscar H.
Hand Weaving with Reeds and Fibers
New York
Pitman Publishing Corp., 1948

Mason, Otis Tufton
Indian Basketry, Vol. 1
New York
Doubleday & Co., Inc., 1904

McKay, Barbara
Basket Making in Pictures
London Daily Mail Publication (n.d.)

Roth, Henry Ling
Studies in Primitive Looms
Halifax, England
Bankfield Museum, 1950

Thompson, W. G.
A History of Tapestry
London
Hodder & Stoughton, XCMVI

Tod, Osma G.
The Joy of Handweaving
Princeton, N.J.
D. Van Nostrand Co., Inc., 1964

Periodicals
Arts and Activities
Craft Horizons
Handweaver and Craftsman
School Arts

acknowledgments

I wish to express my gratitude and appreciation to colleagues and friends who have cooperated by offering help and time to the preparation of this book. For reading my manuscript: Lydia Bancroft, professional weaver; Dr. Robert Cooke, Chairman, Department of Art, Paterson State College; Beatrice Reeve, Head of Weaving, Newark (New Jersey) Museum. For encouragement: Dr. George Sharp, Assistant Superintendent, Public Schools, Montclair, New Jersey. For granting permission for me to photograph student work: Charlotte Lockwood, Associate Professor of Fine Arts, Montclair State College, Montclair, New Jersey; Dr. Joyce Lynch, Associate Professor of Fine Arts, Paterson State College, Wayne, New Jersey. For graciously lending children's work: Helen Blackman, Dorothy Grote, and others. For interest of college students, especially students of my classes at Paterson State College. For the help of Nina Orsini (student teacher). For special assistance: Eugenie Claude, Director of Child Guidance, Public Schools, Montclair, New Jersey; Evelyn Foote, Consultant in Elementary Education, Public Schools, Montclair, New Jersey; M. Adam Salvo, Fine Arts, Public Schools, Ridgefield, Conn.; Dr. Eleanor Delaney, Professor, Graduate School of Education, Rutgers University, New Brunswick, New Jersey.

Sarita R. Rainey